D1431049

PSYCHOLOGY FOR MUSICIANS

PSYCHOLOGY FOR MUSICIANS

by

PERCY C. BUCK

M.A., Mus. Doc. Oxon.
Sometime Professor of Music in the Universities
of Dublin and London

LONDON
OXFORD UNIVERSITY PRESS
NEW YORK   TORONTO

Oxford University Press, Amen House, London E.C.4

GLASGOW NEW YORK TORONTO MELBOURNE WELLINGTON
BOMBAY CALCUTTA MADRAS KARACHI LAHORE DACCA
CAPE TOWN SALISBURY NAIROBI IBADAN ACCRA
KUALA LUMPUR HONG KONG

ML
3830
.B86

First Edition   1944
Ninth Impression 1965

DISCARDED
WIDENER UNIVERSITY

WIDENER UNIVERSITY
WOLFGRAM
LIBRARY
CHESTER, PA

PRINTED IN GREAT BRITAIN

CONTENTS

Dedicated
to
the innumerable pupils
who have passed through my classes
at the
Royal College of Music
London
in the hope of reconciliation
now that the
tyranny is overpast.

PREFACE

THIS book is not, and does not pretend to be, a treatise on Psychology. It is an attempt to help musicians—more especially the music-teachers amongst them, present and future—to realize that Psychologists have many suggestions to offer them, both interesting and important, which can be applied to the Art of Music in all its branches.

Such an attempt, ideally, should obviously be made by one who is both a trained psychologist and a trained musician. But since such an Admirable Crichton does not seem to exist—or in any case has not so far ventured on the task—I hope it will not seem over presumptuous for an amateur psychologist to try to show his fellow-musicians some of the ways in which his own mind has been swept and garnished by the effort to grasp, however falteringly, the facts and underlying principles of Psychology.

It may reasonably be asked why such an attempt should be made at all, since it would seem from the start bound to be somewhat superficial, and conceivably might result in a mere smattering of knowledge and technical terms, which in itself might be a danger and a hindrance to true understanding. The answer is this. Schools which, by accepting the provisions of the 1918 (Fisher) Act—of which the Burnham scale of pay for teachers is probably the most familiar feature—become entitled to be called "approved" schools, must engage teachers who have been through a Teachers' Training Course. And it was ordained that in such a course one of the compulsory subjects must be Psychology. Consequently all of the principal music-schools of the country, which at once instituted Training Courses, were obliged to find a lecturer in this subject. At the Royal College of Music it has been my privilege to give the Psychology lectures from the beginning, and this book, as many old pupils will recognize, is a compendium of the various talks to which they have had to listen.

One personal explanation I should like to make. Originally the book was written in 1939, being finished at Christmas, when the war had lasted some three or four months. As the possibility of publication seemed remote, it was put on one side to await happier times. Owing to the attentions of the *Luftwaffe* it was completely destroyed, together with all my notes, papers, music, and library. That version was altogether more formal and sedate than this one; carefully documented, and full of references and verified quotations. I have had to rewrite it entirely "out of my head", from my memory of the things I have been talking about for so many years; for I have found it impossible, even in libraries, to get at the many volumes I wished to consult. And it seemed best, under such circumstances, to use the kind of language which comes most naturally to me, rather than to aim at a more literary style.

These facts will, I hope, mitigate any feelings on the part of real psychologists that I have treated their subject with less erudition and dignity than it deserves.

My very real gratitude is due to Professor Cyril Burt, who was good enough to read my manuscript and to make numerous suggestions. I have taken advantage of so many of these, that, if there is any value in the book, much of it must be credited to him. But if the trained psychologist finds, here and there, cause to raise his eyebrows, I beg him to attribute the lapse entirely to me, since in a few cases—an instance is the avoidance of such a word as "Kinaesthetic", which would have simplified many purely psychological points—I have been stubborn enough to adhere to my belief that of all the dangerous forms of knowledge that of "blessèd words" is the most insidious.

P. C. B.

LONDON: *January*, 1943

CHAPTER ONE

PROLEGOMENA

THE Sciences, whatever their particular subject matter may be, invariably follow one simple method of development. Each of them begins with the collection of facts, and proceeds to classify such facts until some principle emerges from them which can be treated as a working-hypothesis; and the more often we find that this hypothesis proves to be true, the nearer we are to the discovery of a law.

Psychology developed, as it was bound to do, along these lines, and began by noticing quite ordinary things and striving to piece them together; so that in this state it might be roughly defined as *Organized Commonsense about Human Nature.*

The critical word in the above definition is "organized". And it is worth while to consider how even the ordinary things in life owe far more to organization than we think. If we had not, as children, been taught our alphabet with the letters invariably in the same order, we should probably never have mastered it at all. If, in learning the multiplication-table, we had learnt isolated facts— on one day that $3 \times 3 = 9$, and next day that $7 \times 8 = 56$—we should never have arranged our bits of information into a system. Any child will soon learn how to look out a word in a dictionary, and later on a train in a timetable, because it comprehends the plan; and the reason that most of us Londoners prefer an A.B.C. to a Bradshaw is that we have mastered the somewhat elementary basis of the one, but have been too lazy to master the system of the other.

Thus we arrive at an important discovery of Psychology—one of momentous value to teachers of any subject—that you can count on your pupils doing far better, if you provide them with some kind of scheme or logical connection in the facts they assimilate. The mind that is willing to set to work without a plan of some sort is not intelligent. Ask a boy to mow the tennis-court; he will, before beginning, decide to run the machine either across or lengthwise in parallel lines. Were he to start from just anywhere and zig-zag haphazardly in any chance direction, you would have very serious doubts as to whether his intelligence was normal.

A little thought will show us how all advances come from the discovery of some underlying principle. For instance, primitive nomad tribes wander about, happen on a tract where there is food growing, eat the place bare, and wander off to find another. Then someone discovers that corn grows from seed; so they eat the best and plant the remainder, determining to make a return visit. Later, by another brainwave, they discover that by planting the seed from the *best* corn they will improve the future crop they are counting on; and so the quality of food and the standard of living gradually improve.

Music-teachers should learn from this that even the elements of music ought, from the very beginning, to be based on some principle. In the matter of key-signatures, for instance, I have found numberless students, often quite advanced instrumentally, who had no idea that the last sharp in a key-signature is always, in major keys, the leading note. And quite lately I "supervized" a class of children being taught by such a student. As she told me that she was teaching signatures I asked a child what major key had four sharps: "We've only learnt one sharp G, two sharps D, one flat F, two flats B♭, so we don't know." Surely if there are seven different major keys with sharps it must be easier to teach one rule than to memorize seven isolated facts?

The time arrived when Psychology became too big and broad a subject to be treated as mere organized common-sense. The experimental and quantitative methods used in other sciences were then introduced into Psychology, so that it became a laboratory science, like physiology or chemistry. The reason for the change, both in nomenclature and method is due to the discovery by psychologists—possibly owing to the teaching of Locke—that, when you teach a pupil, the thing you are really teaching, and must make contact with, is the pupil's *mind*. Accepting this discovery it became imperative to inquire into what Mind is and how it works; and perhaps the simplest definition of Psychology is that which calls it the *Science of the Mind*. Every musician, whether performer, teacher, or composer, has to make his appeal to the minds of his fellow-creatures; so he may reasonably expect to make that appeal more effective if he has studied the apparatus with which he has to make contact.

Let us first try to determine what the mind is, and its field of action. Suppose your car is at your front door, and you are going to drive somewhere in it. You take your seat, turn on the petrol, start the engine, and go through all the necessary drill. At the right moment the engine connects with the car and you are moving. You can go on, stop, turn right or left at your pleasure.

Now I want you to notice just one fact: that the car is a machine, whilst you are a mind. The car did everything solely because your mind made it act in that way. No sane human being has ever imagined, nor ever will, that there can, in some distant future, arrive a day when a triumphant mechanician will invent a car which can start itself, run down the street, and turn right or left of its own accord. The directing mind must always be there, separate and disparate from the mechanism.

In a human being, however, the miracle has happened. If we imagine, without any gruesome details, a body that has not yet come to life lying on a couch. It is just a machine, like the car, waiting to be put into action. You started the engine of your car, and it at once became alive and full of potentialities; and if you could start the heart-beating of the body on the couch it too would then be alive. But at some later moment the body, unlike the car, will take direction of its own movements, will lift an arm, or will perform some act of its own accord. It has become "aware", it is conscious, it has performed the miracle of fusing the machine and the directing mind into one; and a mechanism has become a personality.

We may call this directing mind the *Ego*, and the machine—which, being directed, is naturally in the accusative case—the *Me*. In this sense the motor-car consists of nothing but Me; it has no Ego, and never will have one, so the missing element has to be supplied in the form of a driver, separate and apart. The human being is Ego and Me fused into one by *Consciousness*.

Any student specializing in Psychology would be expected at this point to read widely and to think deeply in order to be clear-headed on the meaning and implications of this word. And such reading and thinking—even if not very wide or deep—would be good for, and I believe interesting to, all of you. You would find, for instance, that when we are stunned our consciousness ceases; but that when we go to sleep it seems to be quietly in abeyance, still acting, though out of our control. It is a common experience for one to go to sleep worrying over some problem, and to wake up to find the problem has, as we say, "solved itself"; our mind has been working, as it were, "on its own".

The phrase *Subconscious Mind* has been invented to account for such workings as the above; and it is worth calling your attention to such a phenomenon, as you will find very soon that one of the really important facts which Psychology has to teach you and me is that we shall do our job better—especially the physical part of it—if we trust the machine to do it without the supervision of the mind. All of us, at some awkward moment in our lives, have been quite unable to recall the name of the person to whom we are talking. At last we give it up in despair and go about our business; and straightway the name comes to mind—when we are not thinking of it at all.

For non-specialists it is sufficient to know that when the body on the couch became "aware" and self-acting it had been provided with a

Mind; recognizing that to the Psychologist the word mind does not cover processes of a single type. Nearly every mental process includes three distinguishable functions: *Thinking, Willing*, and *Feeling*.

Nowadays Psychologists have still further extended the field of their study, and find that the last definition—the Science of the Mind—is a little cramping. So you will find modern Psychology has to allow for an enlarged scope. Earlier psychologists treated the processes of the mind as though they were always conscious processes—often, indeed, as though they were exclusively intellectual processes. It is essential, therefore, to realize that feeling and willing are quite as important as perceiving and thinking, and that many of the mind's motives may be wholly unconscious. Such a range must clearly include many things which, however absorbingly interesting they may be to psychologists or in themselves, can add little or nothing to the equipment of a musician. It *would* be interesting to know why, when you are singing or playing at your best, your dog just sits and howls; but the knowledge might conceivably lead to your trying to perform so as to please him, and so the problem may well be left alone.

There are two purely psychological points which are worth noticing before we go on.

(a) Ask any friend what he means by the word "experience", and you will usually get the answer "Something that happens to one". It will be more scientific, and so more true, if you accept the word as meaning, not the event, but your reaction to an event. If you were to overhear someone discussing your character you might feel pleased, or possibly annoyed: i.e. pleasure or annoyance would be your reaction. If you did not quite catch the remarks, your reaction would be curiosity as to what was really said; if you were deaf and heard nothing, then there would be no reaction. Yet in all three cases the event—i.e. the whole occurrence outside yourself—was identical, though you had in each case a different experience. We all start our lives with an inherited disposition: a tendency to react in a certain way; and every experience we undergo adds itself to our accumulating knowledge of how to meet—i.e. to react to—a situation, how to control and conduct ourselves, and how to piece together our experiences into an understanding of life. And all the time we are modifying our native dispositions.

(b) In our very early days, when we are acquiring new data at every moment of our lives, we acquire knowledge almost entirely through the evidence of our senses; and this fact is epitomized by saying that children are *Objective*. It is certainly true that children (a word which means unsophisticated folk of any age) are struck

by the superficial things. It is the plot and the incidents—especially
the accidents—in the story: the brilliant colour or the "anecdote"
in the picture: the tune and rhythm of the piece of music, or the
brass band playing it: these are the things that arrest and hold the
young. And the process of education is very largely a growth and
development away from the purely objective stage, and towards the
stage when the mind can apprehend the meaning and purpose that
lies behind the outward and visible sign. That means, towards the
Subjective, or *Interpretative*.

In the Arts this is specially true. The ingredients of a popular
tune—its rhythm, shape, sequences, etc.—are generally so obvious
as to be almost primitive, and the popular picture is the one that
tells a story (like "The Doctor") or recalls (like "Derby Day")
some event which everyone can take in. It is right and natural that
this should be so, and it would be unpsychological to lament it; all
that is asked of you is to be indignant that, as far as music is concerned, so many millions should make no progress in discrimination
and never discover that music has any meaning at all. For as we
grow up and develope in taste we discover that the plot, the colour,
and the tune, important though they still are, are infinitely less
absorbing to us, because we have also discovered that behind words
and notes and colours there can be a meaning and a motive which
in our early stages we never divined. In every piece of music we
hear, you and I search for this hidden treasure, knowing that it is
the one thing that really matters since it is the one thing which will
touch our hearts. And, in the prosaic language of Science, that means
that we have passed at all events *some* milestones on the road from the
Objective to the Subjective.

If, as I hope, you have grasped the broad meaning of those two words,
one short warning will possibly save you from being somewhat mysti-
fied by their use. At first they seem to be synonymous with concrete
and abstract; and we then think of them only in connection with the
sense of touch. A table is objective because we know it to be "solid".
But you must accustom yourselves to think of the words as applicable
also to the other senses. The full-score of the Choral Symphony is
objective because you can put it on the scales and weigh it; and what
you are weighing would be equally objective if it happened to be any
other symphony. But the Choral Symphony itself, apart from any
copy of it, is also objective because it is in itself a real and recognizable
entity, and would continue to be the Choral Symphony if every copy
in the world were lost or destroyed.

The last paragraph dealt with a point which is at bottom a philosophical rather than a psychological question: i.e. the meaning of the

word "real". For musicians it will be sufficient to realize that we develop from children, who judge by the easy recognition of melody and rhythm, into more sophisticated beings who look for the feeling embodied in the form; from the tune to which our itching feet insist on beating time, to the hidden meaning behind the quiet phrase which once may have seemed so pointless and unexciting. And one of the greatest contributions that Psychology makes to Civilization—which means the education of man in the mass—is by pointing out that all education, in any subject, must aim at grasping the inner meaning instead of confining our attention to the outward appearance. The fact that England produced Shakespeare and Milton does not mean that we are a literary nation; the test of that is the number of us who appreciate the works of those poets. So when you hear a discussion—as inevitably you will, sooner or later—as to whether England is a musical nation—remind the participants that the question is not to be settled by the number and quality of the composers we produce, nor by the percentage of people who "like music", but by the kind of music these people like.

CHAPTER TWO

REACTION

IN learning any new subject, of any kind, you will always find that there are certain new words, or old words with new uses, with which you must sooner or later become familiar. You cannot discuss cricket with a man who refuses to learn the meaning of "leg-bye" or "coverpoint", nor football or hockey if he does not understand "off-side". One such a word, in Psychology, is Reaction. The word was purposely used in Chapter one, in its usual primary sense; but it will be wise to go a little deeper into its meaning before leaving it.

When a man of Science wishes to examine anything at all minutely, his first endeavour will be to get his material into some logical order or arrangement. In the case of an "event"—i.e. anything that happens—the order will necessarily be chronological. How did the various episodes occur, in order of time, and by what nomenclature shall we group them?

The psychologist has devised four classes which will help you to analyse, or to describe, any happening in your life.

1. Stimulus
2. Sensation
3. Perception
4. Concept

Technical terms such as these, grouped in a style reminiscent of the duller kind of school book, are admittedly a little forbidding; but this particular quartet does serve as an excellent introduction to Psychology —especially to a musician—because it does exactly describe what happens in all circumstances, from the most trivial to the most complicated.

Consider an example. You sit writing a letter, and a knock on the door is heard. What has happened?

(1) Something (in this case air-vibrations caused by the knock on the door) has set your aural nerve working; it has been stimulated into action, so the air-vibrations are the Stimulus.

(2) Your nervous-system is so constituted that when a nerve is agitated into action it carries its message to your brain, and "re-gisters" there. Your body is, from the purely physical point of view, a receiving-apparatus, or sensitive plate, for recording the effects

B

made on your external nerve-endings by outside stimuli. Consequently you are said to have received a sense-impression which, conveyed to the brain, is in this case immediately recognized as the sensation of sound. You will readily see that the most obvious information you receive about the outside world takes the form of sensation: one of your five[1] senses must be the channel through which the stimulus reaches the brain. If you were to lose the use of all of them, then nothing in the outside world could get into contact with you. You might still be thinking, but your thought would necessarily be confined to things apprehended in previous sensations. In this instance of the door-knocking, for example, if you happened to be deaf your brain would register no sensation, although the stimulus would be the same, whether you are deaf or not. (So, with all your senses, so far as your mind does not interpret the stimuli, what you perceive may be called a simple Sensation.)

(3) You have now the one concrete fact of sound (registered) in your brain, pinned down like a specimen on a piece of cork; and at this moment the higher levels of your mind come into the arena. The mind's first job is to discover what the specimen is, for there are a thousand different noises that might have set your nerve working. From previous experiences you have no difficulty in deciding, or perceiving, what caused that particular noise, and you are said to have a Percept of it. Had the sound which suddenly arrested your attention been a siren, you would have had a different percept though one of the same nature; for you would recognize that the stimulus had not been the same.

(4) At this point the mind, having satisfied itself as to the origin and nature of the sound, begins to cogitate about it: were you expecting anyone, was it a runaway boy, or possibly the postman? In fact, you begin at once to form conceptions of "what you are going to do about it". There are psychologists who treat these plannings of the mind as Concepts. But it will be safer for you and me to use the word in its more restricted sense of general or abstract idea as opposed to a special example. If you look at a coin you have a Percept of it: if you think of your balance (or overdraft) at the bank you have a Concept. If you only know one Sonata in the world, that constitutes your Percept of a Sonata: but if you have even a nodding acquaintance with twenty sonatas you have in your mind an idea of the Greatest Common Measure of them all, and that is your Concept of a Sonata.

[1]The psychologist recognizes more than five senses: but the popular classification will suffice here.

It is always difficult at first to grasp the exact connotation of a technical term—think how long it took you all to discover exactly what is meant by the word "Binary". And in Psychology, as in Music, there are words in the use of which experts are sometimes at variance. The difficulty often arises from our being overapt to think of things as distributable into watertight compartments, whereas in fact classes of things are liable, like the colours of the rainbow, to overlap and run into one another. Where the overlapping occurs is not of supreme importance to us musicians, but it is always important for teachers to try to fix the point at which different minds diverge. Supposing you were to enter a classroom in any school and unexpectedly play the chord D F B♭. To all present the stimulus is identical; all record the same sensations; their percepts are the same, though varying in clearness of definition— they all, for instance, *hear* three notes, though most of them could not tell you the number. But their concepts will vary enormously. I have tried the experiment, and can tell you some of the answers when the listeners were asked what was passing through their minds:

(a) It's a major chord (fairly often)
(b) It's a first inversion (now and then)
(c) It's a common chord (occasionally)
(d) The top note is B flat (rarely)
(e) It's not in tune (perhaps their ears were sharper than mine)
(f) It's the first chord of "God Save the King" (quite frequently)

The sense-organs, then, are in communication with the sensory areas in the Brain; the Brain receives the sensory impulses; and the brain-areas subserving intellectual functions then, as it were, coordinate and examine the data supplied.

But there is another factor; one of special importance to musicians. At what point does the question of *Feeling* arise? Most people have, at some time, seen a performance by a white-robed dancer on to whom the limelight man has thrown a variety of colours. The "event" to use that philosophical term again, proceeded quite independently of the tints imposed on it, and would have been exactly the same if the varied hues had been omitted; but a new interest and appeal arose, super-added to our enjoyment, due entirely to the colour-scheme. So every human experience is accompanied by a "feeling-tone", which is the result of our reaction to the experience; and a simple example will illustrate it.

Suppose you are sitting peacefully in an armchair, and sounds strike your ear. You have experienced the sensation of sound, and you perceive that it is someone singing in the flat upstairs. If that is always happening you may have learnt how to ignore it; or if you are absorbed in the thing you are doing you may have little difficulty in inhibiting attention to it. In both cases the psychological process is nipped in the bud. But if the singing succeeds in forcing itself on your attention, then innumerable results may ensue. It may be a favourite song beautifully sung: your mind forms concepts about it and you feel pleasure. Or it may happen that your critical faculty— which is one form of the application of concepts to percepts—tells you it is bad music, or full of mistakes, or out of tune; and your feelings will follow your verdict. Always you will find—save in the one imaginary case where your reaction attains the absolute zero of complete indifference—that you either like or dislike a thing to some extent, however small. The psychologist calls these feelings "pleasure" and "pain", and though such words sound rather portentous when applied to cases near the indifference line, yet they are useful terms. If you are not clean you must be dirty, to however small a degree. In the room where I am writing these words there is a clock which ticks loudly enough to be audible, and I wish it wouldn't. It would never occur to me to say, in mentioning the fact, that my experience was painful; but my feeling about it does come, psychologically, into the category of pain, simply because I would, if I could, stop it.

It is not necessary, at this point, that the musician should know more than the bare outline of the physical process by which sensory impulses (i.e. the nerve-impulses from the sense-organs) reach the brain; though later on, in considering instrumental technique, the matter will come up again. But there is one fact which ought to be noticed. When a friend speaks to you on the telephone the vibrations of his voice are conveyed to your ear along a wire; and your voice travels back to him along the same wire. If, for the moment, you look on your senses as five friends—which they are—telling you about something that has happened, their messages came to you along wires; but your messages back have another set of wires to carry them. These body-wires are called *Nerves*, and they are real material things—like thin silken threads, forming a network of communication all over your body. The nerves from the surface of the body to the brain are technically called *Afferent* or *Sensory* nerves; those which, when you have decided what steps to take, carry back a message to your muscles are the *Efferent* or *Motor* nerves.

If you get out of bed and step on a tintack your touch-sense immediately telephones a message along its afferent nerve to your brain which is decoded by your perception into "Right foot big toe on untack". If reflex action, or instinct, or previous experience has not already led to a kind of automatic withdrawal on your part then you consider the case (for however short a moment) and send a message along an efferent nerve to your foot-muscles to remove your toe, and probably another message to your eye, along another efferent nerve, telling it to have a look and see if any serious damage has been done.

It is always the desire of people who analyse things to group them into classes; and it is a useful method of co-ordinating knowledge, so long as it is realized that such classes, with their divisions and sub-divisions, are seldom really watertight compartments. So, in dealing with Reaction, psychologists have agreed that it can best be dealt with under three headings :

(1) *Reflex Action.* This class includes all those purely bodily movements which are performed by the "machine" and are normally outside the control of the mind. If a speck of dust touches your eyelashes then you will blink your eye; which is nature's mechanical method of saving your eye from getting things into it. That is a reflex action. It is possible in some cases—in this one, for instance—to inhibit the action by will-power, if you know beforehand when the test is going to be made. You might, for example, allow me to touch your eyelashes and send an order to your eyelid (along an efferent nerve) at all costs not to blink. But if, taking you unawares, I do it again five seconds later, the reflex will work for a certainty. Such actions, you will readily see, are essentially physiological, and are only tabulated by psychologists to make their classification of reactions complete. They are Native Reactions of the most primitive form.

(2) *Instinctive Reaction.* This is Native Reaction of a somewhat more sophisticated kind since it is, in however rudimentary a way, purposive. From the moment of our birth, whether we are human beings, or kittens, or tigers, we have to face a hundred incidents every day of our lives to which we are forced to react. *How* we will react in any given situation, before we have had the benefit of any training or advice, depends on our disposition; which is the sum total of all the qualities we happen to have inherited, through no virtue or vice of our own, from a long line of ancestors. In recent years biologists have discovered many very interesting things about heredity; but I do not think any one of them would risk a wager on what kind of disposition will appear in the child of any two parents, either in human beings or animals. In the same litter of puppies you will find one that has in-

herited its mother's calm tractability, another its father's pugilistic ferocity. Any one of you may have inherited a maternal grandmother's unselfishness and a paternal grandfather's skill in games; whilst your brother may have had the bad luck to inherit a paternal grandmother's conceit and a maternal grandfather's addiction to drink. We enter the cradle as a mixture of inherited tendencies for which we are not in the least responsible, and all our reactions will be in accordance with them unless in later life we learn to modify them through training and education.

(3) *Acquired Reaction.* The last paragraph may seem, at first sight, to paint a rather grim and gloomy picture of human nature; and not many years ago it would assuredly have been denounced as materialistic, pessimistic, and even irreligious. Nowadays it is so universally accepted as a starting-point for the study of ourselves that it might almost be called the first axiom of any thinker who wishes to look facts in the face. Nor need those facts in themselves alarm anyone, for they imply but one thing: that the whole of our training and education is in reality but one prolonged endeavour to substitute acquired reactions for native ones. It is the simplest of identities: being educated =acquiring reactions which are not native to us. If you were to make a list of all the things you had done in any one day of your life you would be astonished at the overwhelming proportion of them which you would never have done, or would have done quite differently, but for your upbringing. Why did you wash yourself, or do your hair? Why did you refrain from sniffling? Why did you greet anyone with a smiling "good morning", or write a letter to a sick friend, or say please when you asked for the salt, or go and practise your scales? You would have done none of these things if you had been left severely alone when young, and no one had ever taught you the elements of living.

To you as teachers this matter is more important than at first it appears. We are all of us apt to look on a naturally happy and obedient child as "virtuous", and on a quick and clever pupil as "gifted", and to feel aggrieved if we have to teach a slow or difficult child. But wise teachers know that to have the latter kind of pupil is a piece of luck. It is a challenge to them which they should accept gladly. The great minds of the world have not always been more brilliant as children than their companions, and some other teacher exists who would succeed with any pupil you are likely to have. And the challenge to you, that you should see if you can substitute acquired reactions for native ones, is a compliment paid you by Fortune, and you should accept it with both hands.

CHAPTER THREE

HABIT

HABIT and Reaction are closely connected. If you feel certain that a man will behave in a certain way, you say it is his habit. In Chapter Two Reaction in its simplest form was discussed; and before talking about Habit it will clear the ground if we do a little exploring where the two overlap.

Every native reaction follows out a certain chronological course before it is complete. It goes through three stages, called

(1) *Cognition*
(2) *Affect*
(3) *Conation*

These three technical terms should be easy to grasp when it is seen that they refer to the three functions of Mind—Thinking, Feeling, and Willing.

(1) *Cognition* means being aware—generally of a stimulus or sensation. Something has come into contact with one of your five senses, your brain has registered a sensation, and your mind realizes that you have been touched, or spoken to, or whatever it may be.

(2) *Affect* (with the accent on the first syllable) means that the experience affects (accent on the second) you in some way: i.e. you either like it or dislike it, to however small an extent.

(3) *Conation* is your tendency to act with a purpose (as the result of your feeling). The cat has cognition of fish, through her eyes or nose; her affect is so much on the pleasurable side that she sets to work to get at it. You may have cognition of a draught, dislike it, and consider shutting the window—though if it is not a very bad draught, and you are in a very comfortable armchair, the affect may not be strong enough to overcome your laziness, and there will be no conation.

From the above little piece of "bookwork" there emerges one of the fundamental maxims of Psychology: that every reaction is preceded by feeling, and, conversely, that all feeling leads to action.[1] Psychologists, since they want to use words which (being derived from Latin and Greek) will be understood all over the world, are often obliged to avoid "plain English"; and they express this maxim by saying that

[1] The "special case" of Instinct will be referred to later on.

there can be no Impression without Expression, or that every Cognition has its Motor Consequences.

At this point a word should be said about a term frequently used in Psychology—*Inhibition*. To the plain "common-sense" man it might reasonably seem that if you "stop" something from happening then there is no positive action, because no visible movement has occurred. If you think of two tug-of-war teams so evenly matched that there is equilibrium between them, the contestants will not agree that they are doing nothing, since they are straining every muscle to inhibit the other side from attaining its ends. That is a physical example; and for a psychical one consider the amount of energy you have (doubtless) sometimes had to expend in the mere effort to keep your temper. So that in the statement that all feeling leads to action we include the fact that such action may take the form of Inhibition.

Psychologically the terms "Habit" and "Acquired Reaction" are practically synonymous; for every acquired reaction, once it really *is* acquired, has become a habit, and the only habits which are not "acquired" are those which are reflex or native. Since, therefore, all training aims at the establishing of acquired reactions—or, as we may now call them, habits—let us see what Psychologists have to tell us about them.

The first point is this: that you have no right to call any process a habit until it has become *automatic*. You and I were once taught our alphabet, and frequently, at first, made mistakes in repeating it; but there came a time when we could be absolutely certain about it, when we knew that, once started, our tongues would do the rest. At that moment the habit was born. When we were first taught to play the scale of C major we had to think carefully, and often unsuccessfully, as to where the thumb came; you do not have to think about it now, I hope, because the process is automatic. Your arithmetical tables, your history dates, all the data with which education begins, are acquired in the same manner; by thinking, until ultimately you can do it by rote, as it were, without thinking. And you must note specially that in the early stages the thinking is always essential: a baby teaching itself to walk is using its brain as much as a mathematician solving a problem, but, once acquired, the art of walking needs no thinking. All of us, in our early days, had to be told to put our hand over a yawn, or not to sniffle; by now, doing the one and inhibiting the other has become second nature. And it is curious and interesting to note how such conventions are accompanied by an awareness, unformulated and almost unconscious, that they exist for the benefit of other people; for few of us, I imagine, "cover" a yawn in the privacy of our own bed-rooms—though even then the knowledge that a yawn is coming prob-ably gives an incipient start to our arm-muscles in the habitual direction. And in the same sheltered spot I am sure most of you sniffle, when you feel like it, quite unashamedly.

There is one danger, in the matter of habit, which is worth mentioning. When two habitual paths of action begin in the same way but diverge at some point later on, there is always a risk that we may follow the wrong track at the junction. For instance, "going to bed" and "dressing for dinner" do, for a time, involve the same actions; and a friend of mine had to endure much leg-pulling through taking the wrong track "over the points". One winter's evening he went to his bedroom to "dress" for a banquet at which he had to make a speech. The curtains were drawn, so he turned on the lights and began to undress, his mind being occupied with his oration. After a time his wife, fearing he would be late, went up to see if she could help, and found him comfortably in bed, going to sleep.

Many pianists have told me of a musical instance of the same error —a calamity which some of you may have experienced, as I have myself. It frequently happens that some section of a piece of music—especially old music—has to be repeated, and that the composer has provided one ending for the first occasion and another for the second. The nightmare comes when you find that, reaching the end for the second time you miss the cue and have perforce to go back again to be beginning—with the prospect of an eternal merry-go-round from which there is no deliverance.

A very elementary sketch of the nervous-system has already been given. No music-student need pry too deeply into purely physiological processes, but he must now be told a little more as to the function of the nerves in the formation of habits.

In reading the history of some great store, such as Whiteley's, Harrod's, Maple's, or any other, we generally find that the founder began in quite a small way—probably with one shop. When he has mastered the management of this—let us say a tobacconist's business—he trains a manager to carry out his wishes, whilst he himself starts another—say a grocery—next door. In time a manager takes over, while a third business is born, and so on, until there is a complete Universal Stores.

Now the human mind works very much on the same plan. By con-centration on one job it controls the muscles (through the nerves) until the "automatic" moment arrives when there is no further need for mind-control. There still *is* control, but the mind has delegated it to a nerve-centre—Mr. Whiteley's manager—and the mind is now free to attend to other things. When you were learning to ride a bicycle you had to concentrate all your thinking powers on the business; in all your school-days you probably never focused your mind on anything so intensely. But when at last you could say "Now I can ride", the control of your muscles had been handed over to a nerve-centre, and your mind was free; you could take out and light a cigarette, salute a passing friend, or hold conversation with a companion rider. The Psychologist would say that after nerve-currents have been repeatedly sent down the same path to the requisite muscles, those paths become deepened into well-worn channels, and the nerve currents now flow along them automatically, without any need for attentive consciousness.

It is possible for students to understand, and even to be interested in, such information about their bodies, and yet to miss the application of the knowledge to their own specialized work. So here are some of the implications of the above which, as musicians, you should consider.

(1) When an action has become automatic, and has thus earned the title of Habit, the muscles have, as it were, fallen into a rut; they have memorized a method and sequence of action, and will always act in that one way and no other. Think of some little difficult passage which you have thoroughly mastered on your own instrument. You can now play it with ease and certainty, *as* you have learnt to do it. But if you were asked to play it suddenly with a different fingering, there will almost certainly be a catastrophe.

A letter long carried in the pocket acquires such creases that at last it refuses to fold any other way; and it is a good thing to think of habits as having formed a kind of "rut" into which the cartwheels must find a way if things are to work smoothly. French psychologists actually use the word *canalization* to describe the process, and the analogy is one which is easy to follow.

(2) You should now understand exactly what psychologists mean when they say "Do things carelessly". If misunderstood the maxim is clearly dangerous. But it is really a terse and striking way of reminding you that the final end of all practice is the moment when you can do the thing without thinking; when, that is, you can rely on your nerve-centres and muscles fulfilling their task, whilst your mind is care-free. When, however, you have not yet reached the automatic stage—when Mr. Whiteley still has to supervise—the supreme consideration

is the absence of carelessness. Any practice done without conscientious carefulness is a psychological sin; and if it is only just filling in ten minutes of spare time those ten minutes may well cost you ten hours of expiation. It is safe to say that careless practice, with a large number of students, retards their progress to such an extent that hard work can scarcely do more than catch up with it. When you have pupils you will discover the bitter truth that redeeming a fault is far more laborious than instilling a virtue.

(3) You know, and Mr. Whiteley knew, that when a job is once delegated to someone chosen for his competence, nothing but harm can result from your hovering round, putting in a word of advice, and generally killing your agent's interest, independence, and sense of responsibility. So when you can once do a thing automatically, do not allow your mind to interfere; you will do better without it. I remember many years ago—before the days of electric railways—being one of a group of schoolboys who made up a prize (by paying a penny apiece) which was to be won by the boy who could walk farthest along a railway-line. Some only managed four or five steps, some a few more; but one boy negotiated fifty, then turned round and came back. We all crowded round to learn the secret of the miracle. He told us (although I am sure he had never heard the word Psychology) that one day, when he was no better at it than we had proved ourselves to be, he discovered that it was easy to do if you thought of something else; so while he was performing in this competition he had repeated to himself the "thirteen-times-table". We all found, on experimenting, that this was true, and immediately set off in search of uninitiated innocents to provide a purse for us.

We often think that our muscles cannot overcome some difficulty, whereas they can do it with ease, if we let them. For instance, ask any pianist if they can play "two against three" in one hand: "two" with thumb and first finger

then with the three free fingers add

I have often found really good pianists "give it up", yet it is only the mind which finds it formidable. Just place your hand on the table and imagine you are playing this bar—

—and your muscles have done what was asked of them perfectly and without any difficulty whatever.

(4) Many of you have probably regretted, at some time, that you were "nervous", and it may help you to know something about the why and wherefore. In the first place, do not regret it too much, for nervousness is largely an index of sensitiveness, and without sensitiveness you will never be an artist at all. All fine performers are nervous, though they differ in their control of it. When you are completely at your ease you do a thing, as has been insisted on, automatically, through your nerves having control of your muscles. As soon as you are influenced emotionally your nervous control is affected, and your muscles do not work quite normally. Go into the Albert Hall when it is empty and walk across the platform, and your gait will be perfectly normal. But if, just before starting, you had been told there was a large and critical audience waiting to see you walk across and to criticize you, it is quite certain your feelings would be affected and your gait in some way abnormal. You might be amused, or alarmed, or self-conscious, any of which states would mean that your nerve centres, or the co-ordinating centres in your brain, were not able to function quite as automatically as usual in the management of your muscles. If they were seriously affected they would behave as Mr. Whiteley's manager would, in an unexpected crisis: they would send for the Director. So your nerve-centres in such a crisis need your conscious attention—i.e. brain and will-power to come back into control, for there is nothing else in the world that can help you. Such control will become less and less imperative at every repetition, though it may remain (and should remain) essential in some degree all your life. If you realize that you must, for the sake of your artistic value, retain some degree of that self-consciousness which we call "nervousness", and that self-control is the only imaginable cure should you happen, at the moment, to have too much, this knowledge will reduce your sufferings. For if you agree that you have no self-control you must face the fact that publicity was not meant for you.

Professor William James, in his *Talks to Teachers on Psychology*—a book which should be read again and again by every teacher (and parent) in the world—offers five pieces of advice, out of his great experience, to those who wish to acquire any new habit. I will give you his maxims in my own words.

(1) *Start with a flourish of trumpets.* Suppose you determine to get up every morning at 6 in order to put in some practice before breakfast. If you keep that resolution to yourself then, when it breaks down, you will be the only person to know about it; and few of us despise our own personal failures as much as we should. Publish your resolve abroad, let the rest of the household and your friends know of the decision you have made. Then, when tempted to break your pledge, you will be fortified by the feeling that, out of self-respect, you cannot have the finger of scorn pointed at you.

(2) *Miss no chance of putting your resolve into practice.* If you come to the conclusion that you must not use quite so much bad language do not forthwith seek the company of elderly aunts and those amongst whom you would be restrained by mere good manners. Go even more than usual amongst those from whom you picked up the habit, and by an effort of will restrain yourself.

Some years ago a curate told me that a working-man, in whose family he was interested, was taking to drink. The man's excuse was that on the way home from the factory there were seven public-houses. and he couldn't be expected to pass them all. So with infinite pains, and a local map, the curate worked out a new route from factory to home, on which there were no public-houses at all. Now if the curate was acting solely in the interests of the wife and children, this solution has its good points; but if he wanted to reform the man, any psychologist would have told him that his new route should have contained as many more public-houses as could be found.

You may suppress, but cannot eradicate a tendency by destroying its scope of action; in all probability it will, during its temporary restraint be merely accumulating force and momentum for an ungovernable outbreak when the opportunity occurs. You do not cure a boil by putting cold cream on it, however much it may ease the situation.

(3) *Create opportunities.* This maxim, being the corollary of the last, has also been covered by the examples given. But it will provide a piece of practical advice for those of you who suffer from an excess of nervousness. You may find that your ordinary life offers you few

opportunities for acquiring a natural ease and confidence in performance. Then try for all you are worth to discover some way of rounding
up an audience. Offer to perform, even if you have to be a little "push-
ing" about it; collect a few friends whenever you can, and inflict yourself on them; find a pupil and play her pieces to her; ask some children
to tea and play for their dancing. No amount of self-examination and
wishful thinking, whether in an armchair or on your knees, is going to
kill your agitations; nothing in the world will do that except giving
your nervous-system repeated opportunities of fighting and winning.

(4) *Never make an exception.* It is an unkind proviso of nature
that one crime demands many acts of atonement. If you work at a
passage where the difficulty is the fingering, your only chance is to
decide on how you will finger it, and work on it with concentrated
thought until it is automatic. It may mean a thousand repetitions.
But if, after fifty of them you are careless and stumble, you have not
just merely done it wrong for once; you have wiped out all the benefit
derived from probably twenty-five of your trials.

(5) James' final maxim is one which applies mainly to teachers, and
especially to young teachers; and perhaps most of all to those keen and
eager spirits who wish, above all things, to be conscientious and thorough: *Don't talk too much; the "rut" is the goal at which you are aiming.*
It has been my duty for many years, as Supervisor of the Teachers'
Training Course at the Royal College of Music, to watch students
giving lessons, and to write a report on what I see and hear. The
students themselves see these reports, and in them find criticisms of
both their strong and weak points. If I had to generalize about the
reports of about twenty years, I should unhesitatingly say that the most
universal fault is overtalking. I have been to a half-hour singing-
class in which—timed by a stopwatch—the children have actually
sung for no more than seven minutes. Any experienced trainer knows
that in such a class five minutes talking to twenty-five of singing is a
much nearer approach to the right ratio. If you are teaching a boy to
bat you must tell him, tersely, what he does wrong, and why; and you
should show him how, if you can. But if you talk for twenty-three
minutes out of a half-hour at the nets the only possible result will be
inefficiency and boredom.

One last point is of real importance, because it is the basic fact at
the bottom of all that has been said about Habit. *We can only think of
one thing at a time*; i.e. only one idea can be focal in our mind. If you

have ever found yourself talking to your partner at a dinner-party, and have become interested in the conversation that is going on between the pair on your other side, you must have discovered this truth. For a short time, with luck. you may be quick enough, by "shuttling" your attention to and fro, to say "yes" or "no" to your partner at the right moment; but sooner or later your applecart is upset. Try this truth out for yourselves in this way. Sit down and read at sight a piece of music sufficiently difficult to demand your real attention; then get some friend to come and ask you, while you are playing, any simple question— as simple as you like, provided it is not one which you can answer automatically. If your friend were to say "What happened in 1066" you would probably go on playing without disturbance; but if he were to say "What is three times seventeen" I think you would find your playing either suddenly halt or, if you still make the effort to go on, that its accuracy, time, rhythm, and everything else would collapse like a pyramid of cards.

CHAPTER FOUR

THE COMMONSENSE OF TECHNIQUE

THE purpose of the last lecture was to give you some idea, in broad outline, of what psychologists think and say about Habit. And it is more than probable that it occurred to many of you, as you were listening, that to us musicians Habit is closely interwoven with what we call Technique. Certainly that is the case; and I doubt whether there is any section of Psychology from which we can learn more. So in this talk you shall hear of some of the ways in which we can find a practical application for the theories you have heard; since all of us, whether instrumentalists, singers, or composers, work at our subjects with the idea of acquiring that Technique which will enable us to show what we can do when we no longer have to bother about difficulties in performance.

In all the thousands of things which human beings try to do—whether with the mind or the body—it always becomes patent, sooner or later, that some ways of doing a thing are better than others; "better" meaning that, if we master that way, we can have higher hopes of certainty and precision. We cannot, in things which have to be done constantly, invent a new way every time, whether it is boiling an egg or playing a Chopin Scherzo. So, whether it be because we are wise (as optimists think) or because we want to save ourselves trouble (according to the pessimists) we organize and systematize our processes by analysis and experience and call the result the Technique of the subject. To musicians it is scarcely necessary to stress its necessity, since so many of them are rather in the danger of exaggerating it, through not clearly seeing that it is, in essence, only a means to an end. The more skill you have, as you know, the more adequate will be your power of presenting what you have in your mind and heart; which is another way of saying that your power of expressing yourself is limited by your technique.

Let us begin—as is always wise in thinking about words which we habitually use—by analysing the word a little.

Technique may be either Mental or Muscular. Children can do long-division sums—a feat which would probably have completely baffled Julius Cæsar—simply because they have learnt the mental technical process invented for the purpose. Many of you are trying to acquire the technique of part-writing; and the smiles you see on the faces of your teachers seldom arise from their appreciation of your efforts. They are rather wondering if and when your eyes and ears will ever acquire the technical skill which will make you secure from consecutive octaves and false relations. For the present it is unnecessary to say more about Mental Technique, so now we will turn to what is of more practical importance and immediate interest to you: the Muscular Technique necessary for instrumental and vocal progress.

Muscular Technique. In talking about muscular technique one mistake is so common as to be almost universal, and we musicians are amongst the worst offenders. We are apt to talk about "piano-technique", "violin-technique", "singing-technique", and so on, as if the word "technique" meant something different in each case. But our bodily movements are all muscular movements, and there are certain ways of using muscles which are right—for the reason that they are more reliable, are easier in the end, and lead more quickly to automatic action—and other ways that are wrong. These rules, so long as they are fundamentally observed, can be modified and adapted to particular purposes, but they cannot be rescinded.

As an analogy, consider the word "Grammar". It means, roughly, that in an attempt to communicate with anyone by word of mouth men discovered that, in order to be intelligible, certain rules have to be followed. For special reasons these rules varied in different languages, and idiosyncracies of grammar grew up—e.g. in Russian, I am told, the plural is not used until you have six of a thing, because, when people counted on their fingers, five was one handful. But the word "Grammar" means the same to a Russian and an Englishman, independently of any modification in its application to their languages. In the same way you must master your muscular technique, whether your aim is a stroke at cricket, a new dance-step, a back-bracket at skating, or a chromatic scale; and the right way of using your muscles in the one is never the wrong way in the other.

One more preliminary. Many people—at all events, in my experience, many music-students—are so ignorant of their bodies that they do not realize that your muscles are the "lean" of your body as opposed to the fat, and that they exist for the purpose of controlling joints. Leaving aside physiological details about tendons, and about joints (such as the wrist) which will move in many directions, the ordinary simple joint is where two bones come together as if on a hinge. Look at the knuckle of your own first finger. One muscle, covering the joint like a piece of elastic with an end attached to each bone, will lift the finger; another, fixed underneath in the same way, will pull it down.

An anatomist would want to emend and amplify this rough draft in detail; but for you and me, as musicians, it is correct enough for a working hypothesis. A physiologist might prefer to say that all our

c

jointed limbs, such as the forearm, the wrist, and the fingers, are controlled mainly by muscles working in pairs. Thus, to bend a finger, a bending or flexor muscle is contracted. To straighten it, an extending or extensor muscle is contracted. In ordinary health states most of our muscles are moderately contracted: "braced" or "toned up" as we say. But when we deliberately move a joint we sharply increase the contraction of the muscle that bends it, and the opposing muscles are at the same time loosened or relaxed. However, if too much energy is put into a movement the energy is apt to overflow into muscles whose contraction is quite unnecessary, and, indeed, likely to impede the movement we want to produce.

Now we are ready to consider certain rules for the management of these muscles which have been discovered for us by psychologists and physiologists.

(1) *The muscles of a joint can be in any of three conditions: absolutely rigid, absolutely loose (i.e. relaxed), or balanced.*

"Rigid" means all muscles tight, as when you clench your fist.

"Loose" means no muscle tightened in any way, as when you shake your hand to warm your fingers.

"Balanced" means *one* muscle tight, the other loose, as when you lift your arm and hold it at a certain height. As soon as you relax the holding muscle the arm falls, and the "pulling-down" muscle has not been used at all.

When you take your seat at the piano your arms are hanging at your side, and all your arm-muscles are loose. But before you begin to play you have to "manage" six joints: shoulder, elbow, wrist, knuckles, and the two finger-joints. Only one set of muscles is needed to lift the arm from the shoulder to the proper angle; only one to make the elbow-angle as you want it; only one to raise the wrist and prevent it from "flopping"; only one of each pair of knuckle-muscles, to hold the fingers above the keys; but in the two top finger-joints both muscles must be firm and rigid to prevent the joints from giving way when the key is put down.

(2) *Never tighten any muscle except those whose tightness is necessary for the job in hand.*

Whatever your instrument, you must all have been told hundreds. of times—especially in your early lessons—to "loosen" or "relax" In all probability you thought you *were* loose. Nearly every difficulty, however, in any muscular activity, turns out to be, when you have mastered it, merely the discovery of how to loosen certain muscles whose tightness was holding you back. So make sure that you know what relaxing means.

Suppose a pupil is playing the piano to you in such a way that you say "Relax!" Being obedient, she relaxes: which means that her six joints become ungoverned in each arm, and her arms fall quite loosely to her sides. You did not mean the pupil to relax, but merely to loosen certain muscles she has tightened unnecessarily; but how is she to know? Certain muscles *must* be tight, and acquiring technique in any muscular difficulty is always mainly, not training the muscles used, but finding out the knack of loosening the others. For nearly everyone in the world, when they are required to stiffen the up *or* the down muscles, immediately stiffen both. Try this experiment on your friends: ask them to stand up and hold out both arms at shoulder-level. When you say "Drop" they are to let their arms fall to their sides. In the majority of cases you will find the arms hit the sides and stay there; which means the arms never "dropped" at all, but were *pulled* down by the lowering muscles. If the right method had been used the arms would have been held in position by the tightened "lifting" muscle, and on the word "Drop" this muscle would have relaxed, the arms would have *fallen*, and would have gone on dangling against the sides like weighted ropes. In the same way, when you hold your hand as you would in playing the piano, if I were to press the back of your hand slightly it should make no impression, for your holding muscle prevents the wrist from falling. But if I put a finger, from underneath, on the palm of your hand, and pressed it, the hand should rise from the wrist, because the pulling-down muscle should not be in use.

It would be easy to give you the names of all of these muscles; and if I did I suspect that some of you—the information-hungry ones— would conscientiously memorize them all. But that kind of knowledge is entirely unnecessary. I do not believe that any musician ever improved his technique—and it is quite possible that some may even have hindered its natural growth—by knowing that a certain muscle, which you use every time you play a scale, is called the *extensor ossis metacarpi pollicis*.

(3) *When tightening the muscles of a joint, do not allow others to tighten in sympathy.*

It was pointed out to you a little way back that you have six joints to control in mastering anything which employs your arms. And you will remember that "control" means the sending of a telegram along a nerve from the brain to the muscle. Now unfortunately we all suffer from a habit, when a message is sent to a muscle at any distance, of obeying the order with all those joints which come between. Try this on yourself. Lay your arm on the table with all the muscles relaxed; then grasp some object with your fingers. You will be an exceptional case if you do not find that when your fingers tightened on the object, your wrist tightened also. Then try an example on your friends. Ask them to put their arms out slightly in front of them and then to "wring" their hands, i.e. shaking arms with wrists and fingers loose. At a given order they are to clench their fists. When the order is given you will find all of them have stopped "wringing". "Clenching" is tightening the fingers into a bunch, and a very little practice will show you (and your friends) that the order to tighten was sent to the fingers and not the wrist, and that to continue shaking the wrist when the fingers clench is quite easy.

In piano playing this tendency is of real importance, since the chief fault of young players—rigidity—is due to the knack not having been mastered. Many teachers are not aware of the difficulty, and even advanced players sometimes do not know the cause of it. For instance, lay your right arm and hand on the table, and frame the fingers tightly so that they would play the chord

Now consciously loosen your wrist, keeping your fingers rigid, and tap the table thirteen times. Even an elementary pupil would soon acquire ease in doing this. Having got the knack it ought to be quite easy to play the opening of the last movement of Beethoven's Sonata in C major, op. 2, No. 3—

If you were to give the above movement to a pupil without any technical advice, she might labour at it for a week and then bring it to her lesson thoroughly disheartened, and with all manner of faults established which you would have to eradicate. But show her first how easy it is to do on the table, then to apply to the piano with only the thumb to steer, and finally the one snag of the last chord but one being a 6/4 and not a 6/3 (and the possibility, and extra fun, of playing G and A in the last two chords with the left hand), and she will be one step nearer to realizing that an analysis of the difficulty makes all technique ten times easier.

(4) *Improvement in sight-reading means reducing your rehearsal-interval.*

When we perform any muscular action which is to be succeeded immediately by another we are said to "mentally rehearse" the second action whilst performing the first. The orders go down from the brain to the muscles just a little beforehand so that they shall be ready for action when the time comes. There is no deep or difficult meaning in the words "mentally rehearse"; it just accounts for something we all do.

Show these notes, to any pianist in an armchair,

and it is a practical certainly that his thumb and two fingers are alert and ready to pounce on the chord.

It has been said in print—though I hope the experiment is not frequent—that if a hen is running along and you suddenly and unexpectedly chop off its head, it will go on running for a few steps before falling down dead. The nerve-messages ordering those few posthumous paces have left the brain before the head left the body and the process is so rapid that the muscles receive their orders and act on them. Whether this particular instance be true or not, the process is confirmed in many ways in our own lives. When children, in the early stages of reading, see the words THE CAT IS ON THE MAT, they look at T, then at H, then at E, and by an effort of memory say "the", and transfer their attention to C. Each letter and each word is so isolated that the meaning of the sentence is often not apprehended. But if any of you were to read a sentence out loud you would discover, possibly to your surprise, that you were never looking at the word your tongue was actually pronouncing, but always a little to the right. It is the same in music. If you are a really bad reader—in the stage of the child reading about the cat—you look at a chord and play it, then look at the next. But very soon, if you persevere, you find you are never looking at the chord you are playing; and as you improve in your reading you look more and more to the right, your brain having "rehearsed" a number of chords and sent orders to your fingers. If ever you "turn over" for a good player you will be astonished at how far ahead he likes the "turn" to come. On one occasion I turned over for a really good reader who was playing at sight a difficult piano part in a piano-quintet. Before we began I asked him how far ahead he wanted the turn, and he said "about three inches". If the story of the hen is true, it seems quite likely that if this pianist had lost his head—in the objective sense—his fingers would have gone on playing at least some of the three inches.

The importance of all this lies in the fact that so many good pianists are not also good readers. In a roomful of students, who can all play you a Chopin Scherzo, what percentage would you trust to accompany a Brahms song at sight? If you are a slow reader, remember that any-one can read a piece at a bar a minute, and there is no excuse other than laziness for not acquiring speed. If the child, struggling with the cat sentence, were to lament that she would never be able to read rapidly "like a grown-up", you know that she is talking nonsense, and that the speed at which you and I can read English is not due to cleverness or to any special gift. And the same is true, with no qualification, about the reading of music. To confess that you are a bad reader is to confess to laziness. There are few things you could not now read perfectly, given a rehearsal-interval of five seconds, and with a little trouble you could reduce that to four seconds; and if you fix your mind firmly on the fact that it is, as with reading English, the power of having the next chord mentally rehearsed and up-your-sleeve which is the root of the whole matter, then any one of you can become just as good as ever you want to be.

(5) You will remember, I hope, that when talking to you about Habit, I told you two facts: (a) that an habitual action, being auto-matic, is performed without conscious supervision by the mind, and (b) that we cannot think of more than one thing at a time. A very little thought will tell you, however, that we are constantly doing many things at the same time. We can walk, talk, and open an umbrella, all simultaneously. But in such cases of combined actions you will invari-ably find that mental supervision is only wanted for one action, the others being in charge of a nerve-centre. If you could think of ten things that you could do simultaneously, then at least nine of them must have reached the automatic stage.

There is a point of technique, which arises at this stage, of real im-portance to teachers; and it is this. If you think of two things which you can do, each by itself, with perfect ease, the mere act of combining them together—even when both have reached the perfectly automatic stage—is in itself a difficulty, and often a very great one. Every teacher should have convinced himself of the truth of this fact, so put yourselves, here and now, to an experimental test. Close your fists, and extend your first fingers; then raise your arms to the level of your chin, some six inches away from it, with the points of the first fingers just touching—

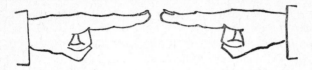

Keeping the left arm still, move the right hand in circles *away* from you. Nothing could be easier. Then, keeping the right arm still, move the left hand in circles *towards* you. Again, nothing could be easier. Lastly, starting from rest, try to do both movements together, always remembering that the right-hand circles are "away" and the left-hand 'upwards". To the great majority of people this feat is so difficult that it is almost humiliating, but with a little slow practice something "clicks" in your mind and you find you have "got the knack", for your mind has found out how to "rehearse" the muscular movements, and to bring the rehearsal-interval down to zero—which means that the whole business has been handed over to a nerve-centre. The practice of such exercises is well worth while even to the most brilliant pianist, for every such knack acquired is one more victory of mind over muscle.

Apply this fact to teaching a child the scale of C major. The child learns one hand, then the other, and the time has come to play both together—a feat so difficult to most beginners that it is almost an invitation to stumbling. And the difficulty lies in three facts: (a) Doing both hands together, a difficulty in itself; (b) using the thumbs on different notes; (c) one hand is "thumb under fingers" whilst the other is "fingers over thumb". Any psychologist would tell you that when the hands are first combined it is far easier for them to play in contrary motion, for then both hands are doing exactly the same thing at the same time, and you are mastering your difficulties one by one.

The "circles" exercise is only one of dozens which can be invented and should be practised for the purpose of muscle-control, and I will tell you now of some more. Master them yourselves, and then make your pupils do them—and I can assure you they will look on them as real fun.

(a) Tap the floor with toe and heel: *one* two | *one* two | etc. Then tap the table with your fingers *one* two three | *one* two three | etc., making bars of the same duration as when you were tapping your feet.

Then do both together. My experience is that any child can learn to do this in a week, and has thereby gone a long way towards killing the bogey of "two against three" which haunted most of us for so long.

(b) Take hold of your nose with the left hand, pass your right hand through the loop and take hold of your left ear. Now suddenly change, taking the nose with the right hand, whilst through the loop the left hand seizes the right ear. This particular exercise has the extra value that it should convince you that, before you can attempt the change-over, you must mentally rehearse the movements you are going to make.

(c) Sit in a chair and, lifting your right leg from the ground, describe circles with your foot as in the illustration—

Keeping it moving all the time, imagine that you are standing at a blackboard with a piece of chalk in your hand, and write a capital D, making the down-stroke first and the semicircle upwards. All organists should master this diffi-culty in all the four possible combina-tions—R.H. & R. Foot: R.H. & L. Foot: L.H. & L.F.: L.H. & R.F., taking care that the direction of the foot-circle is always the opposite to the hand-circle.

(d) Say the alphabet quickly out loud. When you have finished clap your hands to this rhythm—or tap it on the table:

♪♫ ♪♫ ♪♫ ♪♫ &c.

When the rhythm is going smoothly and evenly, start saying the alphabet as before, taking care that it is independent and not in time to the rhythm.

(e) In conducting, as you probably know, the function of the right hand is to give the time, and of the left hand to control expression. Now imagine you have a two-part choir in front of you and the contraltos, on your left, are singing too loudly. Just "hush" them with your left hand. No one could find any difficulty in doing that. Now imagine that they are singing something in common-time, and beat four in a bar for them. Whilst beating time use your left hand to hush your contraltos as before. Any conductor who cannot do this with ease should defer his next appearance until he can.

(f) Endless combinations of movements can be made, when once you can do such things "carelessly". Do the "circles" again, when you have mastered the knack, and add saying the alphabet. Do the "two-against-three", standing at the piano, and with the left hand play "Three blind mice"—and so on.

It is easy to dismiss such proceedings as frivolous and beneath one's dignity. But since acquiring technique means nothing but learning to control muscle by mind until control is superfluous, every new conquest, however unimportant it may seem, is storing power in reserve; and in the case of children, to whom the normal technical exercises are a weariness of the flesh, if we can make the gaining of control a little amusing we are working for the same ends and also lightening a burden from which there is no escape.

When working at Technique, whether muscular or mental, there always comes a point where we have done enough. If we continue, from conscientiousness or compulsion, we shall get no further benefit from our work. Psychologists would say that we have reached "Saturation-point". A sponge will hold a certain amount of water and no more; if you go on pouring water on the top it merely runs out at the bottom.[1]

With human beings, whatever the business in hand, whether mental or muscular, there is always danger in forcing the machine beyond saturation-point; and it is a danger which instrumentalists and singers should recognize and avoid. And luckily our bodies have their own way of calling our attention to the fact—of showing, as it were, the red lamp of danger. In mental work, it is boredom. Your mind has had enough of that particular activity for the present. It may be maintained, and often rightly, that there are occasions in life when one must persist and persevere through the direst boredom, if only for the sake of one's character and will-power; but from the purely practical point of view you are not going to do first-rate mental work

---

[1] The doctrine of the "saturation-point" needs discrimination, and not a wooden compliance. Two qualifications will occur to many readers: (1) In mental and muscular work something often occurs which James calls "getting your second mental wind". If you give up too soon this phenomenon never gets a chance. (2) Some of us, in improving, do not move gradually onwards, but reach what psychologists call a "plateau", stay there for a time, then leap on again, almost with a jerk.

after reaching the stage of being bored by it, and too great a persistence in it may lead to overwork and brain-fag.

In muscular work the red lamp is tiredness. The moment that any suspicion of tiredness occurs your muscles are telling you they have had enough of that particular activity; and though you may occasionally go on working them a little longer without disaster, to do so as a habit is to invite muscle-strain and all its attendant nervous disorders.

But it must not be thought that the first sign of boredom or tiredness is a providential permit to take your ease in an armchair. If you have been working at French irregular verbs or Greek paradigms till you can stand it no longer you can change over to an hour with the Binomial Theorem without any danger of brain-fag; and if you have been practising wrist-exercises till your wrist shows the red light by beginning to ache you are in no peril of collapse if you change over to finger staccato, or any kind of practice which calls into play a different set of muscles.

It is worth while to call the attention of musicians to two smaller points, which are both important in practice.

(1) *Economize your muscular actions*, never using more muscles than are absolutely necessary; and this involves analysing, when practising, any complex movement you may have to make. It not only ensures certainty, through being the easiest way in the end, but it also saves time. Have you noticed how, if your bus-fare involves being given two tickets, the inexperienced conductor pulls out one ticket and punches it, then the other; whilst the experienced ones always pull out two at a time and save, in the course of the day, very many muscular movements? Recently I asked a pianist—a good player—to play the first six notes of "God Save the King" with one finger, all as crotchets:

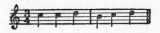

Then I asked her to play it again, putting in between each crotchet the same note two octaves higher. She played each note as before, and in all six cases (1) lifted her hand at right-angles to the piano, (2) stopped, (3) moved two octaves to the right, (4) stopped, (5) put down the note wanted. Five muscular motions for each note. And it can all be done in one by describing a semicircle with the forearm. As certainty of jump arrives, the semicircle can flatten a little into an arc of a larger circle, but the one movement remains. You will find, in all young pupils, a great disinclination to take the hands off the piano, and such an exercise is extremely good for them, whilst incidentally it is gaining arm-control.

(b) Do not expect, and do not allow your pupils to expect, much improvement to come during practice. The Russians have a proverb that we learn to skate in the summer, and to swim in the winter; which is a forceful, if exaggerated, way of saying that it is *between* practices that muscles settle down and, so to speak, assimilate what you have been teaching them.

CHAPTER FIVE

IDEAS AND ASSOCIATION

ONE of the main principles of philosophy, so universally accepted that it might almost be called one of the Laws of Thought, used to be that every happening has a cause. This Principle of Causation, as it was called, has, it is rumoured, had doubts thrown on it in recent years by those who probe the inner mysteries; but for us ordinary mortals it still holds good in the matters with which we shall be called on to deal. If a man falls down in the street the cause may be a weak heart, or a piece of orange-peel, or a birthday celebration; but it cannot be just nothing.

The main discoveries of Science have all been in strict accordance with the psychological processes about which I have spoken to you. Men noticed facts, collected and classified them, and finally someone wiser than his fellows discovered a principle or underlying cause which accounted for them. For innumerable years everyone had seen apples fall from trees, and knew that they always would drop if the tree, so to speak, let go; but Newton was the first human being to see what was the real problem: why do they *drop*? So we got the law of gravitation.

Seeking for the real cause of anything is, however, an elusive business; for there is generally an *immediate* cause, coupled up with a hundred other *antecedent* causes like links in a chain, with an *ultimate*, and usually undiscoverable cause in the dim past. Do not think of such a statement as a learned and solemn theory, for it applies simply and obviously to the most ordinary things. Why are you here to-day? Because the lecture was put down on your time-sheet. Why was it put down? Because psychology-lectures are, by Government edict, part of a Teachers' Training Course. Why was such an edict issued? And a hundred other whys.

As practical people, we shall find that the immediate cause is the one with which we are most concerned, however much we may, as thinkers, be interested in its predecessors. If I were late for my lecture and told you it was because my train was half-an-hour behind time, I am sure you would accept my apology and not ask what had caused the delay of the train.

All action has an immediate cause. If at the breakfast-table you give a little cough, it may be because you have an incipient cold and your throat is irritated; or it may be from nervousness because you have been asked why you came in so late last night; or you may be giving a hint to a brother or sister that they are letting a cat out of a bag; or a dozen other reasons can be imagined. But there *must* be a cause of some sort for the cough. And that cause must be either something *in* your mind or something *outside* of it: i.e. something subjective or something objective. The throat-irritation would be an objective cause, because it would be something definitely happening to a part of your body; the fear of the awkward question would be subjective, because it exists in your own mind and nowhere else. And these subjective things are *Ideas*. The mind is the home, and the only home, of ideas; and the chief inhabitants of the mind are its ideas.

It is usual to group ideas into two classes:

(a) *Mental-Images*, which are the outcome of the experience of our senses. If I were suddenly to ask one of you "Have you ever seen an elephant?" it is a thousand to one the mental-image of one crosses your mind. Even if it did not, you would find no difficulty in understanding that other people experienced mental-images of elephants. But as psychologists you must forget that the word "image" happens to be connected with sight, because you can have an auditory-image, or one connected with any of your senses. For instance, were I to ask you "Do you know the Meistersinger Prelude?" something will happen, if you do know it, though no one can prophesy with certainty what the happening will be. It may be an aural mental-image of the tune, or a visual one of the look of the opening phrase on paper, or (if you happen to have absolute pitch) a recognition of the chord of C major, or (if you happen to have been playing it recently) a tactual one of the feel of the fingers on the keyboard; or even, if your first hearing of it was (as my own was) in the hot and stuffy gallery of an opera-house, a nasal mental-image of the peculiar smell which seems to haunt that region. "Audiles"—i.e. people to whom auditory-images come easily—are very rare, compared to "visuals". Practically everyone can look at a sentence in print (within the compass of their understanding) and see what it means without the help of sound. No one who can read the words KEEP OFF THE GRASS has to say them "out loud" in order to get their meaning. But the number of people who can look at a bar of printed music and "hear" it—again without sound— would form a minute percentage of the population of any country. Yet the acquisition of this power—of the first importance to anyone who takes music seriously—is quite easy to anyone with a little patience and determination. Were you to hand me a lyric, asking if I admired it, would you not be astonished if I said I could not tell till I had read it aloud? Yet if I handed you—trained musicians—an unknown

Chorale, asking if you liked it, I fear some of you would have to admit that you must play it over first.

(b) *Pure Ideas* are more elusive than mental-images, partly because, from childhood, we have always tried to objectify things; that is, to get at a pure idea by means of an example. If I were to ask you, like Pilate, "What is Truth?" you would probably, and a child would almost certainly, answer by giving an example. You might say "We are both in this room". That would be true, but it would not be Truth. The really significant difference between Mental-Images and Pure Ideas is one which I think you will appreciate at once: you have an idea of what a mental-image is, but you cannot have a mental-image of an idea. If you really see the truth of this, then no more distinction should be necessary.

It is a limitation of the mind, as I have already told you several times, that it can only attend to one thing at a time. And the greatest hindrance, as you must often have discovered, to mental progress is that, at every moment of our lives, there are innumerable other things all trying to allure and distract our attention. Psychologists put the fact in this way: our minds are focused on one thing, but there are at all times a few other things on the threshold of our consciousness, elbowing their way into the focus, and a large number of other things in the margin, only waiting for a chance of getting near enough to the centre of things to join in the scramble. And in thinking about mental processes you will find these three words useful: *Margin, Threshold,* and *Focus.* One psychologist suggests that we should think of a country railway-station with a very small booking-office, and a crowd of travellers on a busy market-day, all wanting to buy tickets. The clerk at the pigeon-hole can only attend to one person at a time—the man in the focus who is buying his ticket. But all the time the dozen or so of people who have succeeded in getting into the shed—this is all before the days of queues— are trying to force their way to the pigeon-hole to be attended to; and these are the thresholders. Meanwhile the crowd outside—those in the margin—are fighting their way in so as to gain their ends in or out of their turn. That is an illustration of what is happening in our minds all day long; something or other eternally trying to call our attention away from the thing in focus. In the last few minutes I have noticed that one of you—all the time no doubt trying to keep my words in focus—has shifted her seat twice, apparently feeling a draught; another has uncrossed and recrossed her knees, because certain irritated nerves called for relief; and I myself have been distracted because the pianist above us has played the last note of the third bar of Chopin's Prelude in C minor as E flat instead of E♮.

Complex Ideas seldom lead to action until feeling is aroused. If you pass a beggar in the street you do not automatically give him money, though you comprehend quite well that a gift is what he is aiming at. It is not till some feeling opens your heart that you open your purse. It may be you have just had a tip from an uncle and feel generous; it may be that the beggar is an ill-clad child on a bitter day. Again, you may be sitting one evening in a comfortable armchair finishing a novel, and suddenly hear the clock strike midnight. The idea at once arises that it is long past your normal bedtime, but you will not move until some feeling spurs you to action; a sense of duty, or the remembrance of a promise to go to bed early, which you feel you ought to keep; or even, possibly, the thought of what you will look like to-morrow morning.

At this point it is convenient to draw attention to *Instinct*. There is no need for the music-student, unless he intends to penetrate more seriously into Psychology, to go deeply into what is called the Lange-James theory, but in order that his ideas about instinctive actions may be clear it will be worth his while to recognize two facts :

(1) The first is, that Instinct always implies action. Many of us talk loosely about people being instinctively musical, or of their giving way to the instinct of fear, or of our feeling instinctively that we shall have bad luck to-day. In all these cases we are using the wrong word, and should say "intuitively" or—as in the last case—resort to slang and say we "have a hunch". If someone strikes at you, you raise your hands in self-defence; that is an instinctive action. If you happen to be frightened of cows it would be psychologically interesting to find out the origin of your fear; but it is the fact that you run away when you meet one, and find yourself doing it before you have had time to consider any course of action, which constitutes the instinctive part of the episode.

(2) The second point is, that in instinctive actions such as the above, the action is not preceded by feeling. Indeed, there are those who would say that the acid test as to whether an action is instinctive or not—and there are border-line cases—is whether the action occurred before or after feeling was aroused: though not every psychologist would commit himself quite so far.

It must be remembered that even instinctive actions can be arrested

by feelings arising from some other idea which may be quite unconnected with the main event; and arrested so soon after their start that
they may be said to have been inhibited. If, for instance, just as you
were on the point of running away from that cow, you caught sight,
looking at you from over the hedge, of the face of your dearest enemy,
you might well feel pride enough, though with your heart in your
mouth, to make a more dignified exit.

We come now to a fact which will at once be recognized by every
one of you as something which has been happening to you all your
lives: the *Association of Ideas*. You all know what the phrase means,
and will understand at once why psychologists call it "Habit applied to
Mind". Two ideas (or more) which have for a long time, or on many
occasions, been associated together become so closely connected that
either of them, on entering your mind, invariably calls up the other.
In the textbooks you will be told that there are two ways in which this
associating process happens. If I suddenly say A.B.C. most of you will
find your minds have supplied D.E.F. If I say "Our father" I am sure
the words "which art" have suddenly come into your heads out of the
blue. That process is called *Association by Contiguity*, meaning that the
one has so frequently followed the other that for the rest of your lives
they will be found, as it were, arm-in-arm. This habit is so strong in
some folk that it sometimes becomes an oddity; they can never resist
the temptation to complete a quotation, quite impervious as to its
appropriateness. When I was a boy I remember an old gentleman of
this kind asking my father for his opinion on a mutual acquaintance, and
my father said he was afraid the man was rather a "rolling stone".
Like a pistol-shot the old gentleman said "gathers no moss".

We all depend on association more than we realize. In my student
days I had but one copy of the "Forty-eight" and all my acquaintance with them was made from that copy. And to this day I cannot
think of any one of them without recalling whether it began on
the righthand or lefthand page. When we come to inquire into
"Memory" I think you will see that even such a trifling point as
this has its importance.

There is another method of association called *Association by Common
Factor*. If in the course of your reading you came across a statement
that two things were different "in kind" you might not at once grasp
the meaning; and though it is not particularly subtle it is a matter of
some importance for clear thinking. Philosophers sometimes think
of two opposite qualities as stretching out in two directions from a

middle- or zero-point. Think, for example, of a straight line, and of the righthand end of it as representing very beautiful things, the lefthand end very ugly ones, and all things between arranged in order of merit from the point of view of beauty. As you move from right to left things become less and less beautiful; and there will clearly be a point near the middle where they have just ceased to be beautiful at all and are on the point of becoming positively ugly. That is the zero-point; and the illustration may make it clear why philosophers say that beauty and ugliness are the same "in kind". Similarly virtue and vice are the same in kind, because if one becomes less and less good one ultimately crosses the zero-point and begins to be positively wicked. A child can see that if a thing becomes less and less bright it will not, on passing the point where it ceases to be bright, suddenly become ugly or wicked; though the child does not know the reason to be that both ugliness and wickedness are different in kind from brightness. Yet many verbal jokes are founded on the confusion between things different in kind. Do you remember the man who had dined too well and on his way home asked the policeman " Constable, is this Piccadilly or is it Thursday?"

Such ideas as are the same in kind are said to have a "common factor", and our speech is full of them: rich and poor, tall and short, plain and coloured, and so on. And when you need, especially for purposes of definition or explanation, to get at the exact meaning of an idea in words (often a very difficult thing to do, e.g. with a word like "tonality") it is always a help to ask oneself what is the word's opposite "in kind". A great deal of muddled thinking, for example, about music has been due to the common error of thinking that the opposite to "classical" is "modern".

It is in some ways, perhaps, rather a misfortune that the mind works in this rather prosaic way, mechanically tying up, as it were, bundles of ideas so that we have to recall them with their accretions and seldom really examine them in isolation. But we have to face the fact that the mind *does* work in that way, and a wise teacher will try to discover whether the fact cannot serve useful ends. Psychology is encouraging in this respect, telling us that we can generally break an old association by forging a new one. A schoolmaster once told me of a new boy who came to his school—an English boy who had been brought up in France, and whose normal expression of surprise was, in consequence, "Mon Dieu". Very soon the boy, gradually dropping his French, began to make the same exclamation in English. It obviously had to be stopped, so the schoolmaster—a wise man in his generation—instructed the other boys that whenever the delinquent said "My God" they were

D

immediately to add "fathers". In a short time the boy was cured.
Another example from my own experience may help you when you
are in a like predicament. I once had to teach the piano to a small boy—
learning very unwillingly to please his mother. He had so little aptitude
that when for the first time he tackled the easiest of pieces in G major
nothing would persuade him to venture on to a black note. So I took
to exclaiming "Oh" every time the offending F natural was sounded.
My groans had no effect whatever, so I tried a new ruse; just *before*
he played the note I drew in an audible breath, and the warning worked.
No boy could resist the temptation to score off his teacher, and he came
to connect the look of a note in the lowest space of the treble stave with
my preparations for a groan, and very soon the cure was complete.
But he told me, many years afterwards, that the note F sharp was still
linked in his mind with an incipient cry of pain from me.

CHAPTER SIX

INTEREST

IN speaking of Native Reactions I pointed out to you how we are all born with a certain set of tendencies—good and bad, useful and dangerous—which, in their sum-total, constitute our dispositions; and that, were it not for training and acquired reactions, we should, in a civilized community, be in a sorry way. All these natural idiosyncrasies involve certain natural interests. You, personally may have been born with the interest, spontaneous and unforced, in music: but you may have a sister who positively dislikes music, yet adores painting, or mathematics, or foreign languages.

In the early days of Psychology there was a great belief—a belief not without a valuable element of truth—that the proper course in educating any child was to discover its natural interests and to work on these, and in its way this idea was unquestionably a great step forward in educating; and certainly one cannot deny that our learning progresses with greater ease and speed in those subjects in which we are interested. But there are other considerations which these believers forgot, and three of them are worth thinking about.

(1) In youth we are "sensational", and interested mainly in concrete things; as we grow up we become more and more intellectualized and interested in ideas. People tell me that nowadays every small boy, asked what he wants to be when he grows up, would choose some branch of engineering, owing to the novelty and attraction of cars, motor-cycles, aeroplanes and wireless—none of which even existed in my own schooldays. But a very large proportion of those boys will have found, by the age of twenty, that their interests have shifted on to something quite different: mathematics, or medicine, or music. Hence it would be clearly unwise to pin down a child to a plan of education founded on tastes which we know will, in a large percentage of cases, change even before the plan chosen is completed.

(2) One of the greatest benefits we confer on a child by educating him—in the opinion of many thinkers immeasurably the greatest of all —is not the actual learning and accomplishment he will attain to, but the fact that he has acquired the power of working, and working properly, at something which, if left to his own free choice, he would never have wanted to do at all. As things are in this world, it is rather a sad reflection that only a minute fraction of the population are ever going to spend their lives doing those things they are hankering to do.

You yourselves will seldom have the chance of interpreting great music to audiences who are hungering for it; unless you are a great deal luckier than most musicians you are much more likely to have to spend innumerable weary hours, whether in health or no, teaching music in unalluring surroundings, often on almost unendurable instruments, to pupils who are mostly ungifted and frequently have no personal desire to learn. Your one and only chance of survival, the one condition on which you can come out of it all still sane and inspiriting, is that at some time or other you have learnt that, once a job has been taken on, for your soul's sake you must put in your best work at it. I am not emphasizing the moral side, though the moral side is obviously there; but rather the psychological fact that if once you condone slipshod work in yourself you have become, to everyone who falls within your sphere of influence, not an educator but a contagious disease.

(3) Education does not imply, as will be discussed in a later chapter, *knowing* a lot of things but *being* a certain kind of person. And in the case of artists of any kind this is truer than of most men. A writer may have mastered the technique of prose or poetry, but if he fails to be interesting, why should any one read him? You may have mastered the technique of your instrument, but your power to grip your audience depends not on your amazing technical display—that only astonishes—but on your power of being interesting. And "being interesting" comes, not from spending the whole of your life down the one byway of music, but from your having made yourself into a certain kind of person by spreading your wings and getting into contact with great ideas wherever and whenever you can find them. The minds and souls of all the great thinkers and artists and teachers of all time have been moved by ideas which they have placed at your service, and every hour that you spend in the company of the great minds must, unless you are incredibly nonabsorbent, make you a more interesting person, and, *ipso facto*, more worth listening to as a performer.

Interest is always active. This saying of the textbooks, at first sight and in cold print, may look to you arid and academic. But it conveys a truth well worth remembering: that when once you are keenly interested in a thing you always want to be "at it", and resent being kept away from it. By itself this statement may merely seem to mean that if once you get keen on lawn-tennis you are always wanting to have a game; but it includes the more important fact that if, at a given moment, your interest is actively engaged on a thing then it overrides other interests. Try to imagine the greediest boy in the world, to whom the intervals between meals are just one long weariness. If he is once really interested in solving the last clue of the crossword, or finding the piece for some curiously-shaped hole in a jig-saw, then you will ring the gong in vain.

There are two kinds of Interest: *Immediate* and *Mediate*. The former covers those things in which you are naturally interested for their own sake, the latter covering those things which by themselves would not appeal to you, but have become interesting for some other reason.

With all of you I may presume that Music is an immediate interest, but there must be some of you who detest the actual labour of working at technique. You know, however, that you eagerly desire to improve: that you cannot improve without developing your technical equipment: that you have reached your present stage only by such work, which fact has given you faith that you can go further by the same means: and so you come to be interested in doing it for ulterior reasons. Probably each one of you possesses something—a book, a photograph, or a ring on your finger—not specially interesting on its own account, but highly prized by you personally because of some association. That is "mediate interest".

If your nursery days included any French fables, you may remember the pathetic little story of Jeannot's Knife. Jeannot was a peasant boy, devoted to his mother, who once gave him a clasp-knife—a simple contraption of wooden handle and steel blade. Soon afterwards she died, and to Jeannot the knife—his only inheritance—became almost a sacred symbol of her, from which he would never part. The blade wore out and was replaced, and then the handle wore out and another took its place, and by the time he was an old man both had been many times renewed, and not a particle of the original knife had existed for many years. But his last dying command was that they should place in his coffin "the knife my mother gave me".

Arising out of Mediate Interest is what is sometimes called the *Law of Interest*: that dull things can always be made interesting if we can find the way to link them up with things which make a natural appeal. It is a truth on which men have acted since time began, without knowing that they were psychologists. Many practical instances can be thought of with ease. Why do you think there were marks and prizes at your school if it was not to get work out of you by enticement? Did no teacher ever play the old gambit of saying how pleased your parents would be if you came out top in some subject—such as French irregular verbs—which you found particularly wearisome? Or appeal to your pugnacity by saying that surely you would never allow so-and-so to beat you in form-order? Innumerable boys who loathed the subject of Geography have been made keen about it by being given a stamp-album; and people who detest railway time-tables find they acquire almost a halo when a holiday journey has to be mapped out. And have you not still a remnant of that special interest which all children feel in things that are their "very own"?

The late Mrs. Curwen, a most remarkable (and lovable) woman, and a great teacher, once told me that in her early days she taught two sisters, and gave a volume of pieces to the elder, writing the girl's name in it. The younger girl—the more gifted of the two—needing a new piece, was told (for economy's sake) to learn one from her sister's volume. To Mrs. Curwen's surprise the child seemed to lose all interest in her work until, after a great deal of bother, it was wrung from her, with tears, that she wanted a piece that belonged to herself alone. A new copy was provided, and the sun came out again.

When you look around and think of the things at which your various grown-up friends work with energy and zeal, you will be surprised at how many adult enthusiasms are really secondary, or "mediate". If your father is a surgeon, you cannot imagine that he ever derived immediate pleasure from cutting anyone with a knife; so why does he do it? And think of how many girls and women in recent years have given up most of the things they like to eat and drink, solely from un-willingness to let their weight increase. Children, however, being sensational, are interested almost entirely in immediate results, and cannot look far ahead. You may get a child—though I am very far from recommending the experiment—to practise scales by placing a piece of chocolate on the piano, to be eaten when the clock strikes; but a glowing prophecy of how well she will play in two years time will not move her to any great resolution. With intelligent grown-ups, however-the motive-power of most of our actions is foresight.

In reading about Interest you will probably, some day, come across the statement that "Interest is rhythmic". Such a saying is apt to be accepted, by the unthinking, as merely academic, or even a little cryptic. But it means no more, and no less, than this: that "being interested" is not a stable state of mind, but rather one that ebbs and flows. If you are a good teacher you may succeed in getting your pupils interested in their work; but you must be a better teacher still to keep them inter-ested. Do not make the mistake, so natural to young teachers, of think-ing that your really valuable work is amongst your gifted pupils, and

that the rank and file are just an unfortunate necessity which you have
to suffer in order to earn your living. Almost any teacher, except a
miraculously bad one, can get a talented pupil to improve, for really
talented pupils teach themselves and need little more than a guiding
hand. The real measure of your success will be the number of those
whom you raise from the mire, where, but for you, they might have
stayed. You and I know how great music can open the windows of
heaven; and you must realize that, to the majority of your pupils, the
only possibility of ever getting a glimpse into Paradise depends on you.
So you must try, above everything else, to make your lessons of such a
kind that your pupils' interest will flow of its own accord, and then to
forge links which will carry them over the inevitable ebb that will
follow. Never, by any chance whatever, give a lesson unprepared, for
that is the first unbreakable law of all good teaching; and if, in spite of
every effort, you fail to arouse that curiosity which is the outward
sign of interest, do not despair—either of the pupil or yourself—because
it is beyond doubt that there exists a teacher somewhere in the world
who could succeed, and there are still many ways you have not tried.

Not long ago I heard an experienced teacher say that every lesson
should be a complete entity in itself, a little microcosm, self-sufficing
as a chapter in a book. And I could not help wondering that he should
have been led by experience to a conclusion so different from my own.
If ever you have read a serial story you will know how it is the business
of the writer to end his instalment with words which will make you
impatient for next week's continuation: "in fear and trembling she
opened the door and was confronted by a sight too terrifying for words"
(to be continued next week). In the same way you can end a lesson by a
challenge. If, for instance, you have initiated a pupil into the mystery
of the dominant seventh of C, you can say "See if, by next week, you
can find out for me the dominant seventh in any other key. I *shall*
be surprised if you do."

To supplement what I have told you about Interest, I should like
to give you two maxims, and to urge you to think about both of them a
good deal. They are not to be found in any text-books, but both are, I
believe, of real importance to any student who wishes to grow in wisdom.

Maxim 1. *Any fool can do the thing that interests him*, though not
necessarily in a first-class way. The point of the maxim is, that if you
honestly desire to improve you must not keep on doing the things for
which you have a flair, but must find out what you are bad at, and
hammer away at that. If you want to improve at lawn-tennis, but
know your backhand is the weak spot, do not take the righthand court

and shout "Yours, partner" every time a backhander comes along; nor, if you finally *have* to take it, run round it to turn it into a forehand stroke. Go and practise backhanders against a wall until you are fit for good company. If you love playing Chopin and Liszt, but know that Bach and Scarlatti expose your weaknesses, do not always try to cajole your teacher into giving you something romantic. Work at the thing you ought to be able to do but cannot, and work until the secret comes, as come it will. And if you do, not the least surprising result will be your discovery that your work at Bach has improved your Chopin out of all recognition.

Maxim II. *It is your duty to be interesting.* This may seem a hard saying to those sensitive and shy people who are conscious of a difficulty in winning and holding attention. But there *is* a solution, and you may learn it from a true parable.

When Horace, the Roman poet, was an old man, the young poets came to him on his birthday and read an address to him, couched in terms of flattering courtesy. Would he tell them,they asked, how it was that he could touch people's hearts, so that they themselves could learn his secret. In his reply Horace told them that there was only one way of touching men's hearts, and that was by showing them that you had touched your own.

Do you not realize, whoever it may be talking to you, that the moment he becomes eager and shows his obvious absorption in the matter, you yourself cannot fail to be interested. Cannot you recall some one teacher, from your schooldays, who could hold you spell-bound? What could be the source of that electricity other than the teacher's enthusiasm of the moment? I have known teachers who could come here and hold your attention in talking about a quaver-rest; but it would only be because, in talking about it, they themselves became really interested. For it is difficult to think of anything in the world in which a wise man could not interest himself by seeing it " *sub specie æternitatis*": not in isolation or as a transient thing, but in its relationship to the great whole of which it is a part. Remember, then, that in order to be interesting only one condition is necessary: that you must show that you are interest*ed*.

CHAPTER SEVEN

ATTENTION

ATTENTION is usually defined as the *Concentration of Consciousness*. There is always something in the "focus" of the mind, however tenuous our hold over it may be; and until it has been ousted by one of its competitors from the "margin" we are said to be "attending" to it.

There is one point in connection with this which all teachers should grasp at the start: that once the spell of your attention is broken it is extraordinarily difficult—with children one might almost say impossible—to recapture it—i.e. to replace the same idea in the focus of your mind. If you are telling your best story, with everybody "all ears", and in the middle of it something distracting occurs—the dog and the cat start a fight and have to be separated, or the chair of the heavyweight guest suddenly collapses—you know how impossible it is, when peace and calm have been restored, to pick up your story again with the words "As I was saying". Consequently, if you happen to be talking eloquently to your class about the mysteries of Compound Time, and suddenly the Alert sounds, necessitating ten minutes in the shelter, you should, when you come back again to the class-room, finish off your lesson with anything in the world except Compound Time.

There are two kinds of Attention: (a) *Spontaneous*, and (b) *Deliberate* or *Volitional*.

(a) *Spontaneous Attention* is sometimes subdivided again, and is said to be either *primitive* or *intellectual*. This means little more than that the object of your attention is appealing either to your senses or to your mind: i.e. it might be labelled as objective or subjective. Even the baby in the perambulator will find its attention immediately arrested by a barrel-organ or a brass-band; and the danger of allowing our mental attention to be distracted, or even destroyed, by some phenomenon presented by one of our senses is a danger that persists through life. However absorbing the sermon, the spectacle of a cat walking down the aisle will break the spell of attention in the most devout. However magnificently you are playing or singing one uncontrolled sneeze in the audience is fatal. And both of these accidents would be illustrations of primitive attention.

Intellectual attention is when, given that the interest is spontaneous, the concentration of the mind beats the appeal to the senses. If, for example, you set a mechanical toy in motion it is the visible movement that interests the child (primitive), but it is the mechanism that appeals to the grown-up—he wants to know how it works (intellectual).

(b) *Deliberate or Volitional Attention*—the power of concentrating on a thing not in itself natively interesting—is probably the greatest mental asset of any we can possess, for without it progress in things of the mind is impossible. And it should be a real encouragement to you to learn that, in the opinion of all psychologists, it is acquirable— unless you are prepared to admit that you are totally devoid of will-power. So you should one and all seriously take yourselves to task and determine that, at any cost of personal convenience, you will go in quest of it.

Innumerable people will tell you, self-excusing themselves for their poor attainments, that they never could concentrate; and the statement is invariably untrue. All of us have, usually to an unlimited extent, the power of spontaneous concentration. When you have just finished the last chapter of an absorbing novel your attention has been so completely occupied that you will hear with surprise that someone has been asking you questions without getting an answer from you. And you could probably not only describe every detailed incident in those fifty pages but could say whether any one of them occurred on the righthand or lefthand side of the page. If, in your schooldays, you had acquired the power of reading fifty pages of history in the same way, think, not only of the amount of knowledge you would have stored in your mind, but of the toil and worry you would have spared yourself. And you would also have won one more victory of mind over matter.

Invaluable as is the power of Deliberate Attention, the teacher must never forget that, *in a lesson*, it has to be eliminated. If your pupil, or your class, is obliged to "pull itself together" in order to attend to you, then there has been something amiss in your method. You can never expect that all your pupils will come to your room with the eager light in their eyes betokening that they are hungry to learn; but they are nevertheless, like all human beings, ready and glad to attend to anything which interests them. Still, there will be occasions, whether your fault or theirs, when the difficulty of securing their spontaneous attention will seem almost superhuman. In such a quandary the psychologist can offer you three pieces of practical advice—you can call them "tips" if you like:

(1) *Change the subject.* In America, where they are fond of making experiments with large masses of people and tabulating the results in the form of percentages, some psychologists set out to discover how

long the normal human being could be trusted to keep his mind fixed
on one thing and one thing only, keeping the object focal and undis-
turbed by marginal ideas. The verdict, i.e. the average result after
thousands of experiments, was, I am told, almost exactly eleven
seconds. The tests were, of course, always those in which deliberate
attention was necessary; when the attention had to be consciously
focused on something—such as a brassheaded nail on the wall—
which was in itself uninteresting. You can easily make the experiment
on yourselves. Fix your mind on one of your fingernails, or the electric-
light bulb, or a patch on the carpet, determined to concentrate on it
like a cat watching a mousehole, and see how long it is before you find
some marginal idea has elbowed its way into your mind.

Most of you will probably admit that the chord of the dominant
seventh is not in itself a thing of spontaneous and absorbing interest,
and that you do not expect any of your classes to find it so; and this
implies that, when you are telling a class about it they will be
obliged, about every eleven seconds, to jerk themselves back into
attending to what you are saying. Yet only recently a young teacher
said to me, with not a little pride, "I gave my whole lecture to-day
on the dominant seventh". I cannot help wondering whether her
satisfaction with herself and her feat really equates with the feelings
of the unfortunate class that had to undergo the penance.

(2) *Challenge their intelligence.* Real teaching is not "telling", it is
making them find out; and even if they fail, or find out wrong, more
good than harm has been done, because the habit of using the mind
has been strengthened.

Recently I "supervised" a class in which a young teacher was
initiating some small children into the meaning and function of a
dot after a note. It must be allowed that the most gifted teacher
might find it difficult to radiate interest over a dotted crotchet; much
may therefore be forgiven to an inexperienced beginner. But she
ought to have been sensitive enough to "feel" the complete boredom
that permeated her class. It was imperative to relieve it, so I asked
the children what they thought a "dotted sixpence" would amount
to, and they were at once alive again.

Some day most of you will have to take a class in what is, curiously,
known as "aural training". The word "curiously" is used because the
sole object of such a class is, at bottom, to train people to listen, and
listening is not done with the ears. "Listening" is the application of the
mind to the sounds which the ear—a purely physical organ—may or

may not hear. If I say to you "Was that an Alert" you all immediately listen; that is, you focus your minds into a state of readiness to deal with the evidence of one of your senses, if it happens to occur. Your ears do one thing only: they "hear sound". That means that something from outside your body has attacked you and made your machine work: you have been put in the accusative case by a stimulus from outside. When you "listen", however, you are in the nominative, for you are focusing your own mind by your own active efforts (will power) on something presented to it. So do not think it an unimportant truth that hearing is a function of the ear, whilst listening is a function of the mind.

In most Aural Classes there is too much "telling", and too little mind-training. You all realize, for instance, that in fine music the important "part" or "line" of the music is not necessarily the "treble" or top part. You know that it is an essential condition of appreciating Bach that one should take in the inner parts. Yet even amongst fully trained professional musicians the number of those who are really good at hearing inner parts is astonishingly small. If you take a really well-known and simple tune, and write a treble part above it and a bass underneath, you will be surprised at how few of your musical friends can "spot" the tune. Here are two examples to try on them, in case you suspect me of underestimating their ability:

Even with a class of quite small children you can begin a training in listening with elementary examples, such as the one given below. You should collect a store of similar specimens, and might well spend a few minutes on them at the end of any class—especially one where the interest has shown any signs of lagging.

You will find, in giving such tests, that you are teaching your class genuine concentration, you are training them in a habit essential to musicianship, you are making a refreshing change from something which, however essential it is, they may have found a little dull; and you will find that the children enjoy it as much as a game—which it is.

A lesson which was given to my form at school when, as very small boys beginning Latin, we were being introduced to the Accusative Case, is worth recording as an example of challenging intelligence. Our master had a puppy named Pickles, well-known to all of us, and he was training it to keep to heel. He had explained the accusative case to us in words, as well as he could, and probably feeling that we were not very receptive about it, he said he would tell us a story about Pickles, and we were to correct him at once when he used any word wrongly. "I am training Pickles to walk behind me, and he *will* keep running in front. So I got a little whip, and told him that the very next time he ran in front I would hit he." With one accord we all shouted "him". He then explained that "him" was simply the accusative of "he", and that curiously enough we should find that in Latin accusatives also ended in "m". That was "challenging our intelligence" and nothing else; and I am sure you will realize that we learnt more in two minutes than many hours of "instruction" would have drummed into our heads. You may say the man was a "born teacher", and so he was. But of the best teachers I have ever known I think the majority were not the "born" ones, but those who had made themselves excellent, as you may, by study, experience, and humility. And the greatest of these is humility.

(3) *Always be prepared to switch to something which employs the senses.* Sir William Ramsay, the great scientist, told me once that sometimes he found, in his large classes at University College, that the attention had dwindled to zero. It might be the end of term, an exciting football match that afternoon, or a dance in the evening. So he always carried a piece of string in his waistcoat pocket, and at a crisis would stop talking, take out the string, and slowly and carefully manipulate it, as if about to make a "cat's cradle". He said the effect was always

instantaneous. Every student followed everything he did with it. And when he quietly replaced it in his pocket they recognized the silent rebuke, with a little self-conscious amusement, and he had their attention once more.

So you will find, as an application of the above ruse, that in your teaching most of the things you merely *say* about music will fall on stony ground, unless the sense of hearing is brought into play. If, for example, you are struggling with the difficulty—a very real one at a certain point in the teaching of theory—of getting your harmony class to use second-inversions properly, there is nothing that an angel from heaven could say that will really get into their heads the one and only point of the whole trouble—i.e. that when we hear a 6/4 chord something in our minds tells us that the bottom note is a dominant. It is more than likely that most of you are entirely unenlightened by that statement. But if I play two simple chords, of which the second is a 6/4 you know at once that something at the back of your mind is begging for an F sharp.

It sometimes surprises teachers that, in their lessons and lectures, they must aim at eliminating this Deliberate Attention, in spite of the great importance we rightly attach to Concentration. So let me add at once that it is the one habit above all others that you must try to establish in your pupils' work. Practice done without concentration is a psychological sin for which, if your aims are serious, you will sooner or later pay dearly. If you had realized at school that your progress depended, not on the number of hours you gave to your work, but on the intensity with which you applied your mind to what you were doing, you would have saved yourself many dreary and wasted hours, and would find that to-day you had less leeway to make up. When once you have discovered that real application—a word which implies determination—had resulted in the mastery of something which once you could not do, you will find (and I am sure some of you must already have experienced the delight of finding) that what began with effort has become a sustaining desire. You actually enjoy making the effort of application because you have tasted the joy of conquering difficulties. Bishop Gore, of Oxford, whose whole life had been connected with education and centres of learning, was once asked to make some generalization about students, from his great experience of them. And he said that the most striking and unexpected discovery he had made was that, although the natural gifts of people varied enormously, yet he was convinced that such differences in talent were of little or no account compared with the question of what a man does with whatever talent he possesses.

One more psychological point is worth noticing, because it has a direct application on all teaching. When a person's natural interest and attention are aroused by undesirable things, how can you change them? And for this purpose psychologists suggest two cures :

(1) *By grafting on an over-riding interest.* Enough has been said in Chapter Six on this point. We will all, like athletes in training, gladly forgo a pleasure for some end we really wish to achieve.

(2) *By gratification.* This form of cure may seem, to the sterner moralists, to lack austerity, but if it succeeds in its end it needs little apology. I am told that the manufacturers of biscuits and sweets allow new hands to gorge themselves to their heart's content, knowing that in a short time repletion will safeguard their goods from further depredation.

I once had a boy to teach—in redemption of a promise to his mother—who rather dismayed me at his first lesson by saying that the only music in the world he had any use for was "rag-time"— the popular poison of the moment. So we came to an amicable understanding that we should take it in turns to choose his piece, with the stipulation (to which, in his surprise at the concession, he agreed and adhered) that when he chose his ragtime he should work at it seriously. He won the toss, and really tried to master his piece technically; then I chose a simple and tuneful bit of Schumann. For about a year we went on like this until one day, when it was his turn to choose, he turned to me and said, rather plaintively, "Please, sir, *must* I play any more ragtimes?"

Even if you have found nothing in what I have said about Attention which seems to you to be of any special importance, I should like to fix firmly in your minds one maxim which is possibly the most important single fact that Psychology has to teach you. You will remember my saying that the mind is always attending to something. If, therefore, you ever allow yourself to say that your class was inattentive, you are simply saying what is not true. They *are* attending to something, and your remark is merely a public confession that they found something else more interesting than they found you. Surely that is not a fact to publish from the housetops. Do not, as so many teachers do every day of the week, lay the blame on them, but commune with your own soul and try to discover why and where you lost hold over them, and allowed their minds to wander. They are under no vow or obligation to attend to you, and you are being paid to teach them—i.e. to gain and hold their attention; so that you will admit there are many teachers in the world who are earning their living on false pretences. It would not be a bad thing if every teacher in the world were to have hanging in his bedroom, so that it would be seen first thing every morning on waking up, a motto framed and glazed like the texts of an older generation; and the words would be: "If ever my class is inattentive, it is because I am dull."

CHAPTER EIGHT

MEMORY

EVERY musician will be ready to admit the importance of Memory, and should therefore be glad to clarify his ideas, possibly a little vague and unorganized, as to its nature and possibilities.

The first point to be recognized is this: that Memory is of two kinds (a) *Recognition*, (b) the power of *Recall*. We frequently meet people who attribute the want of success in their school careers to their having a "bad memory"; and they will not readily believe that this plea is seldom or never true. Practically everybody has a good memory in one of the two classes named above, though very few, in my experience, have excellence in both. The mere knowledge that you are weak in one category and strong in the other should spur you on to repair your deficiency, and I believe you will find that Psychology can help you.

(a) *Recognition*, sometimes called *Memory Proper*. You will remember that I have already pointed out the cardinal difference between ideas and sensations: that you can, for example, have an idea of a smell, but not the smell of an idea. Memory deals with ideas—sometimes, of course, prompted by sensations—and Recognition occurs when an idea presents itself, and we recognize that we have met with it before; or when we meet with an object—i.e. have a sense-impression—and the idea occurs that it is not our first time of meeting.

(b) *Recall* happens when we search in our minds for something, and the idea comes up to the surface; often making an apparently instantaneous appearance, but always chronologically subsequent to the first moment of search. You meet your father in the street; you see his face and figure, *then* recognize him as someone you know; having done that you then recall who it is. It is all done in such a small fraction of a second that we are apt to think of the whole event as one and indivisible. In the same way, if I strike a certain triad of notes on the piano you will all say "Major common chord, root position" and it only took a minute fraction of a second for you to discover the fact. But think of the many things which happened, all in chronological order. (1) My fingers struck the keys, (2) the hammers hit the strings, (3) the strings vibrated, (4) the air took up the vibrations of the strings, (5) the air-vibrations travelled to your ear-drum, and thence to the sensory end-organs in your inner ear, (6) the stimulation of these end-organs caused currents of nerve energy to travel up the auditory nerve to the brain, (7) when the currents reach the auditory areas at the side of the brain, sensations of sound are heard, (8) when the nerve-currents travel across the association-paths to the appropriate speech-centres, and so down to your lips and tongue, you utter the phrase "common-chord".

Our power of Recall depends, primarily, on the Retention with which nature has endowed us; and the retentiveness of different people varies very widely. You may remember the simile of the "Rut" which was used in discussing muscular habits; and you will find it useful to think of your power of Retention as working in the same way, applying, so to speak, the law of Habit to your mind.

But Nature may have given you poor powers of retention, which you wish to improve; and improvement can be ensured by the expedient of coupling ideas together; for memory is always a nexus, or linking-up, of two or more things. As William James points out, if someone suddenly confronts you and says "Remember!" your mind is a blank. You can only remember *that* A *is* B; *that* two and two make four; *that* your name is Mary; *that* the knot in your handkerchief was intended to remind you to do some special thing—though in my own case the discovery of such a knot so often led to a long and vain effort to recall what it was for, that I have abandoned this particular form of mental nudging.

The above paragraph is in reality just a roundabout way of stating that, to a psychologist, Memory is practically just a convenient synonym for *Association of Ideas*. You associate 1066 with the Battle of Hastings, and, having made the nexus when you were young, you have succeeded in retaining it. You connect some quite arbitrary number with your telephone or stores-ticket, and if your retention is good the number sticks. If you have learnt a piece of music by heart, always playing from the same copy, I am sure that most of you, in playing it, uncon-sciously remember where the "turning-over" places come.

If such associations are made in early youth, when your brain is plastic, they will last apparently for ever. I can tell you now, with cer-tainty, what was the number of my father's stores-ticket sixty years ago; but to save my life I could not tell you a single figure in my own, and I have to carry it about with me. All of you, probably, can remem-ber some occasion when a chance sight, or word, or even smell, has suddenly brought to mind a fact or incident, perhaps of long ago, which you had practically forgotten. A friend of mine, who has some rough shooting, used to go round it with the "keeper" at the end of the season, to "clean things up". On one occasion they were crossing a bridge over a stream, and solely to make conversation my friend said

"What do you think is the nicest way of having your breakfast-egg done?" Before the man could answer some birds got up, and the desultory conversation was forgotten, with the question unanswered. A year later, cleaning up again, they were crossing the same bridge, in silence, when the keeper suddenly turned to him and said "Poached".

There are several points in connection with memory which will well repay thought—more especially as at first you will possibly be disinclined to accept some of them as true.

(2) *You cannot improve the retentiveness with which you are born.* But before you are seized with depression let me add that you can improve your powers of memorization, almost without limit, by developing your association-systems.

(2) *Improvement in one association-system does not affect another.* That is, however much you may develop your system in one particular line, you will not thereby improve your normal memory in other lines.[1] There are, for instance, men whose memory—say for scientific facts— is so colossal that one does literally wonder that one mind can hold such a vast amount of information. But if by chance you know such a man, you know also that he is the last person to trust with a letter to be posted, and that his wife would be quite astonished if he remembered his wedding-day or her birthday. Again, if you were to determine to learn by heart ten lines of Shakespeare every day you would certainly find that the time taken for the task grew less and less. You might, in a month, reduce it from twenty minutes to five; and you would probably feel that you were "improving your memory". But you will find that you take just as long as before to memorize a piece of music or a list of history-dates.

(3) *Interest is of supreme importance.* We have all known boys who, though good at games, are perilously near the bottom of their forms— "because I cannot remember dates and irregular verbs and things like that. My memory is so bad". Yet such a boy will generally be able to tell you, in the summer term, the average of every leading batsman from a mere cursory glance—not a study—of the newspaper average-lists. If I mentioned the name of a piece of music to a group of pianists— say Beethoven's Sonata Pathétique—and asked them to say something

[1] This is perhaps not quite exactly true. Twenty years ago, or so, few psychologists would have expressed belief in "transfer of training". Nowadays there is a little more readiness to admit the possibility under rare conditions.

about it, they would think of many things. The solemn opening, and
the very look of it on the paper; the key of the slow movement; the
time of the Rondo; and a dozen other things, which they have never
had to "memorize" at all, would crowd into their minds at once. But
it would have been a wearisome and laborious task to learn all these
things if they had not been interested in music.

(4) *Artificial aids to memory are not always to be despised.* There is a
tendency to label all adventitious helps to memory as "cramming",
and then dismiss them as evil. Without suggesting that cramming is
the most desirable form of learning, it is possible to say something in its
defence, since any artificial help is necessarily a form of cramming—
being a substitute for learning a thing outright. When you learnt your
notes, were you not told that the spaces in the treble stave spelt the
word FACE? That is cramming; and it would be mere pedantry to say
it was a bad method of helping you to remember. In my club, recently,
a friend and I met at the pegs where we hang our coats, which are num-
bered. He walked straight to the peg where his coat hung, whilst I was
searching rather hopelessly for mine. I asked him how on earth he
managed to remember his number, and he told me that generally he
had to search as I was doing, but that he had noticed, on hanging up
his coat in the morning, that the number of his peg was twenty-three.
Youthful memories came to mind and he had said to himself "The
Lord is my shepherd". Your generation, they say, does not know its
Bible, but I trust that most of you will decipher the association in that
story. It is, all the same, an example of cramming of a primitive and
elementary kind.

There is one characteristic of cramming, seldom recognized or
acknowledged, which justifies a limited and reasonable defence; it is
that, although you are relying on an auxiliary crutch for your power of
recall, there does arrive a moment when you have assimilated the fact
and can discard the crutch. As a boy I found it extremely difficult to
remember dates, so I had recourse to a system which was common in
those days. You convert your figures into the corresponding letters of
the alphabet, and then make up a sentence in which those letters each
begin a word. When we were doing the Elizabethan period, for instance, I wanted to fix the date 1588 in my mind ; so I took the letters
AEHH and invented the sentence "All England howls Hallelujah".
The connection, as you see, stayed in my mind, but it was not long
necessary for me to recall the sentence in order to remember the date
of the Armada.

In matters which are "off the beat" of our real studies such aids to memory are often useful and pardonable short cuts. To you and me Astronomy is not a subject on which we wish to spend much time; nevertheless it is desirable for any educated person to know the names of the planets. Their names and order, starting from the Sun, was planted in my mind by a sentence I was made to learn as a schoolboy— the futility of the sentence being one of the reasons one remembered it— "Men very easily make jugs serve useful needs". Again, I do not now have to think of the sentence in order to recall the names of Mercury, Venus, the Earth, Mars, Jupiter, Saturn, Uranus, and Neptune. And anyone who wishes to remember the order of the colours in the Solar spectrum (or the Rainbow) has only to learn the word VIBGYOR (Violet, Indigo, Blue, Green, Yellow, Orange, Red).

You should be on your guard by recognizing the fact that mental memory, like the muscular-memory which we call Habit, may sometimes let you down when two diverse things follow the same path to a point, and then diverge. As an example, you will all know the two tunes "Home, sweet home" and "The bluebells of Scotland". One of my children, when quite young, used to amuse me, quite unintentionally, by constantly singing the "Bluebells", but on reaching the last line invariably ending with "Home, sweet home". A man to whom I related this incident supplied me with another instance—which is also an intelligence test, as some of you may not see the point. He told a friend he was going on business to Melbourne, but knew nobody there. "What luck", said the friend, "I know a man there who is the life and soul of the place. Just introduce yourself as my friend, and he will give you the time of your life. He has the unusual name of Crummack, so write it down." "No, I needn't write it; I shall remember a name like that easily." He then repeated to himself (saving your presence) "Crummack, stomach; crummack, stomach"; sure that he could rely on the association. Many months afterwards they met again, and on being asked how he had enjoyed himself in Melbourne he replied "Very much indeed; but I couldn't find anyone who knew your friend Kelly".

Everybody would like to have a good memory, and to improve the one they possess, however satisfactory it may be. And to that end psychologists offer you two pieces of practical advice:

(2) When trying to get anything "by heart" employ as many of your muscles and senses as you reasonably can. You must surely have discovered that if you have to learn a speech from Shakespeare the quickest way is not just to sit in a chair and read it. Say it out loud, make the appropriate movements with arms and face, try to simulate the sequence of the moods. You would have taken months longer—

perhaps years—to learn your Alphabet if you had never said it out loud; and I think most of you would still be uncertain, like myself, of the number of days in each month if you had never learnt the jingle which begins "Thirty days hath September". Few, if any, singers can learn to sing a song properly by memorizing it in an armchair; nor can you master the fingering of a difficult passage by just learning it off from the book. In both cases you must bring into play the muscles which are going to be used, in the knowledge that, sooner or later—another case of habit—the muscular memory will be free from the domination of the mind. "Finger-memory" is just another case of "doing without Mr. Whiteley"; and I expect that all of you, if asked to write out any piece of music you know by heart, would before very long find yourselves drumming on the table with your fingers, in order to find out the next chord.

(2) When the thing to be remembered consists of a number of facts, try to find some principle running through them—some thread, as it were, on which to hang your beads—before you begin to try to learn the separate and individual facts.

A musical example of this piece of advice occurs in teaching Key-signatures. Even nowadays, in spite of the general improvement in teaching, one often finds children—sometimes even students in the more august musical institutions—who know their keys up to three or four sharps and flats, but beyond that are obviously only hazarding a guess. If you once grasp the nature of a tetrachord you soon "tumble" to the fact that, in major keys, each new sharp is added to the signature solely to provide the new key with a leading-note; consequently, in the sharp signatures, the key-note is always a semitone above the last sharp. Similarly—you can work it out for yourselves if it sounds erudite in words—in the flat-keys each new flat, being the topnote of the lower tetrachord, necessarily becomes the key-note of the next key. In 2 flats, for example, the E flat has to be put in to create the lower tetrachord of B flat major— B flat, C. D. E flat. When you leave out the upper tetrachord— F. G. A. B flat—you are left with the top half of the scale of E♭. Thus in flat-signatures the last flat but one is your Tonic. If you understand this, you give your mind one infallible principle to work on, so logical that you will never forget it, instead of fifteen isolated facts to store in your memory, each one of them—especially to a child—easily forgettable.

Most psychologists, in writing about Memory, add an interesting paragraph on *Forgetfulness*. Pushed to its logical conclusion the act of recalling a thing—if we had to remember what happened at every moment between the event and its recall—would take as long as the gap happened to be. But for the merciful gift of forgetting, or ignoring the things you do not wish to remember, it would take you twenty-four hours to recall what you were doing at exactly this time yesterday. This thought is interesting, and a little humorous, seeming almost to rehabilitate what we usually look on as a regrettable human failing. But it has considerable importance, in that it led psychologists to make experiments as to the rate at which we forget. In one experiment, for instance, a large number of people were persuaded to learn a piece of nonsense-poetry—after the manner of "'Twas brillig". Each of them, on becoming word-perfect, was sent away and asked to appear again at specified intervals, so that it might be discovered how much they remembered. It was roughly calculated that, on an average, after half an hour half the poem was retained; after eight hours, one third of it; after a month, one fifth. If you were to make a corresponding graph you might call it the "Graph of Forgetfulness"; and there is a valuable lesson to be learnt from the steepness of the curve in its initial stages. For it shouts the information to us that we must reinforce our efforts as soon as possible. In practical language it tells us that half-an-hour's practice every day of the week will be far better for us than three and a half hours on any one day, because we are catching up with the forgetfulness of muscle or mind at the point where the deterioration is more rapid. There are, admittedly, some people who need "warming up"; they do not really settle down to work for ten minutes or so; and in such cases the subdivisions of the time available must be made with intelligence. But if you find your pupils are allotted an hour a day for practice I think you would be wise to arrange for two half-hours, as far separated as possible, in the case of nearly all of them, and invariably, I venture to say, in the case of children.

CHAPTER NINE

APPERCEPTION

YOU will recall that, in the last chapter, we discovered that there are two kinds of Memory. The first, Recognition, is sometimes called *Objective Memory*, and has been said, in the unpoetical language of the textbooks, to be due to *Contiguity of Impression*; the second, which is Recall, is *Subjective*. In case you still do not feel quite at home in the use of these two words "objective" and "subjective", and think it strange that the former should be applied to mental things—for we can "recognize" a similarity in ideas—let me again remind you to free your mind from the conception of an "object" as something necessarily material and solid. In everything about which you think there is always the "thing known" and the knowledge about it—whether it is a cathedral or a crotchet rest: and the "thing known", pinned down for examination like a butterfly on a cork, is objective, the ideas about it are subjective.

All of us, I suspect, have at some time felt the temptation, on acquiring a new technical term or phrase, to parade it in public, sometimes to confute an antagonist unfamiliar with it, sometimes merely to display our erudition. I hope none of you will succumb to this ignoble lure by hurling the word Apperception at anyone's head. It really carries a simple meaning which, so far as you will be concerned with it, may be almost exactly expressed by the homely and humble word "twig". But this latter is a word whose connotation is only nicely comprehended by the English-speaking races, and thinkers prefer a word which, from its Latin origin, can be grasped all over the world. So remember that, for all practical purposes, if you "twig" an idea you "apperceive" it.

Apperception deals with new things, which we interpret in the light of our previous ideas; that is, by arranging our ideas into groups, on some principle of connection and relationship, we try to "place" a new idea. We all have, in our minds, little bundles of ideas, accumulated from infancy, stored as it were in pigeon-holes with a label outside. The moment I say the word "Dog", you at once find it quite easy to focus your attention on to all the knowledge you have ever gathered about dogs since you first saw one. If I were to throw on a screen a picture of a miniature lapdog, followed by one of a huge wolfhound, you would know immediately that each of them was a dog. If I were to say I am now going to talk to you about "Sport", another pigeon-hole in your mind is opened, full of ideas about every game you know.

Or if I said the one word "Sonatas", a third group of ideas immediately comes into your consciousness.

These groups, or clusters, or nuclei of ideas are called, in learned circles, *Apperception-masses.* There was once a time when the word Dog meant to you solely the one household specimen of your home. Gradually, from your perambulator, you became aware that there were other specimens in the world; your idea of the connotation of the word expanded and your cluster of ideas grew. No stranger from another world, who had never seen a dog, would readily believe that a tiny pom and a large St. Bernard had anything in common; but your apperception-mass of dogs has grown to include both without hesitation. Those of you who know any philosophy will probably already be thinking of the Platonic Idea, and will see that you have, in the course of your life, built up a conception of dog which, though a distillation, as it were, from the specimens you have met, is nevertheless not a mental-image of any actual and individual animal.

The first important point about Apperception is this: that when a new idea is presented to our minds it immediately tries to find the group, or pigeon-hole, to which it belongs; and until it succeeds we have not "apperceived" it. When I was a schoolboy the Yale lock was invented, and a friend showed me what you would all immediately recognize as an ordinary latchkey, and asked me what I thought it was. Having never seen one before it was, of course, a complete puzzle, and the nearest guess I could think of was that it might be a Jew's harp. You can, I am sure, follow the process. Something unknown was trying to find, in the storeroom of my mind, some cluster of ideas with which it had a common denominator; failing to do so any attempt to classify it became mere speculation.

A second point is this: that when a new idea has found its pigeonhole it necessarily modifies our conceptions, which before the new arrival had been derived from specimens met with up to that point. When it became clear that what the school friend showed me was not a Jew's harp but a latchkey, then for the rest of my life my idea of "Latchkey" was modified and different. If your idea of "dog" was at one time founded on the experience of a single fox-terrier, then the moment your neighbour's collie gained admittance to your apperception-mass your idea of dog had to become the greatest common measure of the two specimens. And that is the way in which all your conceptions of everything under the sun have grown, ever since the day you were born.

One further point is of special importance to teachers. In the cases mentioned above our ideas of the meaning of the labels on our mental pigeonholes have gradually evolved through the modifications made by new ideas. But there are cases where, by taking thought, we can discover logical conditions which will enormously help us in our apperceptions, and make many other things—memorizing, for instance—infinitely easier. There are some wonderful folk in the world, as you probably know, who are said to know their Bradshaw by heart. Ask them the time of a train from somewhere to anywhere and instantly they have an answer. But they have not, as you might imagine, memorized all the trains in the book; they have discovered the underlying principle—a mystery to you and me—on which timetables are compiled.

It is often a matter of astonishment to me to find that quite good pianists, though they may "finger" well enough, have often never apperceived the principles of fingering. In an examination in piano-teaching, for example, any of you might be asked where the thumb comes in playing the scale of E flat major, and I am sure you would all say, without hesitation, "on F and C in the right hand, on G and D in the left". But if the examiner asks "Why not the other way round?" he very seldom receives an answer which proves that the fundamental principles of all fingering have been grasped.

Philosophers have often lamented that the real bar to progress in this world is not ignorance, but "knowing wrong". It does not enormously matter if a given child does not know that two and two makes four; but if the child is cocksure that it makes five, then there is danger ahead. And one of the outstanding difficulties for all teachers is the finding of words which will make one's meaning unmistakable. No mere words can bring a realization of a thing comparable with that to be won by an experience of it. Think of the impossibility of explaining the word "blue" to a man born blind. All the best teacher can do is to give examples—to hold it under the pupil's nose, so to speak—until the moment suddenly arrives when, by a flash of intuition, he "twigs" what we are driving at; until, that is, the moment of Apperception arrives. Supposing I said that so-and-so was a "vacillating" kind of person, you would all know exactly what I meant; but there was a time when that word was not in your vocabulary at all, later on a time when you heard it and wondered what it "meant", and lastly a time when you apperceived it so completely that it became a word you might use at any moment. There are many such words in music, and I expect that some of you have not yet completely twigged all of them. Are you quite certain of the exact meaning of the word Tonality—bearing in mind the wise man who said we have no right to say we really understand a thing until we can explain it to someone who doesn't?

The English language presents a special difficulty for teachers in that we have, from ancient times, refrained from giving a new thing a new name, preferring so often to give a new meaning to an old word. Half the words in our language, as foreigners complain, seem to have a secondary meaning as well as a primary. I remember hearing a rather strange incident described, when someone remarked "That's rather a tall story"; whereupon a French lady, who spoke English quite well, turned to me and said "How can one story be nearer to the ceiling than another?"

In music endless confusion arises, especially in the minds of the young, from this laziness of invention. We talk of major and minor keys, but also of black and white keys; of the notes of a scale and the notes on a page of music; of a "bar", when we may mean the perpendicular bar-lines or the notes between them; and the words "major" and "minor" are used to refer to characteristics of keys or to size of intervals. I remember my own dumbfounded amazement, when I was told, in learning the elements of theory, that intervals were counted from the bottom note upwards, and proceeded to apply the method to chords. I found, in the case of the first inversion of the chord of C *major*, E. G. C., that it consisted of a *minor* third and a *minor* sixth from E.; whereas if you made it into a *minor* chord, E flat G. C., your two intervals from E flat both became major. To you and me now it is all understandable, but it can never be really wise to bewilder the young.

Mrs. Curwen once told me that, having taught a young pupil that 3/4 time meant "Three crotchets in a bar", the child went home and happened to find her mother playing Handel's *Largo*. Anxious to air her new technical knowledge the child said "What time is that in?" When the mother said it was 3/4 time the child looked at the music. "It can't be, mother; why, the very first bar has a dotted minim, and not three crotchets." Mrs. Curwen used to tell that story as an illustration of her own carelessness in forgetting that children are literal, and have an embarrassing way of believing exactly what you tell them. Always remember the child who was sure she knew what an "average" was; "it's the thing hens lay so many eggs on". And make it clear that bars in 3/4 time contain notes *to the value* of three crotchets.

This "literalness" on the part of all children—and a great many grown-ups—is a characteristic which no teacher can afford to ignore. It does not arise from stupidity, but from the commonsense idea that your words mean precisely what they say. Psychologists dignify this fact by calling it the *Law of Economy*; which means that so long as the words are seen to mean *something*, then that will do. Words cannot always be expected—especially by the young—to make sense; indeed, if at school you ever had to battle with translating Cæsar, you may recall the surprise with which you occasionally found that a sentence meant something you might have said yourself.

Many amusing examples of errors due to this Law find their way into those sagas of Master Malaprop known as "schoolboy howlers"; and it is often amusing, and should be instructive to any teacher, to trace where the train of thought went off the lines. Can you follow the mind of the child who said an Optimist was the man who looked after your eyes, while a Pessimist attended to your feet? A volcano, said another child, was a mountain with a hole on top, and if you looked over the edge you could see the Creator smoking. An old Inspector tells how he was once examining a Church school at Bonchurch, a village in the Isle of Wight, where at that time most of the Solent pilots lived. He asked the children to recite the Creed, and every one of them, at a certain spot, said "Suffered under the Bonchurch Pilot". One more example is worth giving as a warning to you to avoid the rather slovenly speech with which so many English people desecrate their mother-tongue. The Vicar of a country parish told me he once visited his Sunday school just after Christmas, and asked a class if they could tell him the meaning of the word Epiphany. Every hand at once went up, with fingers flicking; and he asked a child in the back row, who immediately said "Railway porter". All the hands at once went down, clearly satisfied that the answer was correct. Being naturally puzzled, the Vicar afterwards asked the teacher if she had explained the word. "Certainly", she replied, "I told them it was the Manifestation." "Man" they knew, and also "Station", and the Law of Economy did the rest.

It is possible that, to some of you, all that I have said may seem to amount to little more than that there is a danger of people getting hold of the "wrong end of the stick". But there is more to it than that; and I would like to give you one more example, not in any spirit of humour or flippancy, but as an illustration of how this habit of interpreting words at their face value may, through a child going wrong over one little word of two letters, endanger and jeopardize the happiness of a household. A young married couple had a small daughter who never gave a moment's trouble, and was everything any parents could wish. When the time came for her to use a pencil, it was noticed that, though undoubtedly righthanded, she invariably transferred it to her left hand, as soon as she was alone; and in those days lefthandedness was not approved of. In spite of all commands she persisted in the habit as soon

as supervision ceased. The parents, terribly worried at this first dis-
obedience, could get no explanation from her, until one day, the father,
to whom she was specially devoted, persuaded her to give her reason.
"I do it because God does it", she said. And when asked what made her
think that, she explained "He *has* to, because Jesus Christ is sitting
on his right hand".

The deeper importance of Apperception, however, lies in its implications. Here are three reasons why psychologists pay so much
attention to what at first sight may seem a little obvious and trivial:

(1) *Stereotyped Apperception-masses* create a danger to which we are
increasingly liable as we grow older. You must often have heard it
said—and in later life you will realize the truth of it—that ideas which
are considered "dangerous" in your youth become out-of-date back-
numbers by the time you are old. Even the most conservative of you
(in a non-political sense) have, I am certain, ideas on such things as
socialism, marriage and divorce, or education, which, though they
seem to you merely normal, and not in the least "advanced", would
nevertheless have shocked your great-grandparents beyond measure.
In my early student days we were sternly discouraged from even
talking about Wagner; it had to be done surreptitiously. He was, we
were told, an iconoclast, a heretic in art, an evil influence; and his music
was a "medley of wrong notes". Have you, in these days, heard no
echo of such things from the greybeards of to-day concerning modern
music? Meanwhile, Wagner has became so respectable that, in a
lecture on "Modern Music", I doubt if his name would be even mentioned. And the cause of the opposition in both cases is exactly the
same—ossification of the apperception-masses. Some despondent Psychologist—and I do not think he was very far from the truth—has
averred that the average human being lived for the rest of life on the
conclusions reached by the age of thirty. In fifty years time music,
whatever it may be like, will certainly be something radically different
from what it is now; for change is the essential condition of life, and
neither music nor human beings can keep alive by stagnation. So it
becomes a crucial question for each one of you: are you going to fix
your opinions by the age of thirty, and repeat to your grandchildren,
once again, all the old abusive and abortive criticism of anything that is
new, and in consequence does not conform to your ideas? A great
thinker once said "When you tell me you have a conviction, you are
merely proclaiming that, on the subject at issue, you have given up
thinking". So keep your apperception-masses fluid and assimilative,
dread stagnation of idea like the mind-poison which it is, and make

it a matter of conscience that the whole furniture of your mind shall be periodically examined and refurbished.

(2) The highest aim that I can put before you as musicians is that you should further the cause of good music. It is not derogatory to the human race to say that the number of people who are born capable of recognizing and liking the best straightaway is negligible, if it is not actually zero. The power to appreciate great music is not a gift, it is a reward. Most people, it is true, are susceptible to the superficially attractive things; to rhythm, to tune, to diminished sevenths, and the sound of the trumpet. But they have a long way to travel before they will get the genuine thrill from the Forty-eight. It will be your business to build up their apperception-masses, helping them day by day, and term by term, to discover that there is something in great music which does not deny them the qualities they long for, but keeps those qualities in place and proportion, combining them into a unity never to be found in music of the baser sort. Your enemies, in your musical life, will not be those who do not care about music, nor even those who hate it, but those who love it but like it bad. If in your lives as teachers you can bring even a few of these last over into your camp you will have proved your mettle, and may well ignore the Gentiles without the Law.

(3) Lastly we have a purely psychological consideration: *All Ideas lead to Action.* On this text I have already preached to you. It is brought up again because at this point I want you to see that your every action— especially action in any sort of crisis where rapid decision is involved— will depend on the character, quality, and quantity of the ideas you have gathered together in your apperception-masses. An "able man" is not just a man who can do his job well so long as it follows a normal routine. In giving that title we express our belief that he would not be found wanting when things were abnormal; we think he could cope with a new situation. It is the man whose masses have petrified who stands gaping and hesitant in an emergency. If you have to choose between two pupils, and were told that one was gifted and easy to teach, but the other rather a difficult problem, I wonder which you would choose. For myself, merely to satisfy my own interest, I would choose the latter invariably. Never allow yourselves even to begin to despair when you find a pupil who "beats" you. Heaven has sent you a golden chance of calling up and applying every device your ingenuity can suggest. Grasp it with both hands, not merely for the pupil's sake, but because your own value for life will be raised to a higher power by every

problem that you surmount. So you must keep your minds open and acquisitive, continually enlarging your masses in every possible way, in order to face and cope with the many challenges which will beset your paths as teachers.

CHAPTER TEN

EXPLANATION

A TEACHER has many duties. Amongst the humbler of them is the duty of imparting information; amongst the higher, and probably the highest of them all, the duty of getting their pupils to see the principles underlying facts. You will have to hammer away, using every illustration and analogy that your ingenuity can muster, until the divine moment comes when the principle is apperceived.

The practical outcome of this truth—and I hope you accept it as a truth—is that every teacher will succeed or fail mainly in accordance with his powers of explanation, for it is only by this means that he can prise open the intellect and imagination of his pupil. You will remember, I hope, the instance I gave you, in an earlier talk, of the schoolmaster teaching the accusative case; for it is a perfect example, hallmarked by the fact that in it the pupils did all the thinking.

There are two kinds of knowledge: knowledge from the inside and from the outside—by apprehension or synthesis. Bergson gives us an excellent example. If you have never been up in an aeroplane, he says, and want to know what if feels like, you can ask a dozen people who know from experience. Each account given you will bring you a little nearer to the idea, and after comparing and combining all you have been told—i.e. by synthesis—you may imagine that you have almost got the feeling. But the very moment you step into a plane and ascend you have suddenly acquired a real knowledge of how it feels, an apprehension of the whole matter which you could never have distilled from a thousand descriptions. And Bergson calls that the moment when you have had a "flash of intuition".

All teaching is an attempt to bring the pupil to the point where this flash occurs; and though it comes more quickly in the case of the clever pupil, there are few except the wilfully stupid who cannot attain to it in anything which you are likely to be called on to teach; and even the wilfully stupid are vulnerable to interest.

The meaning and application of all this should be clear if you recall some idea that you have definitely apprehended, think how long it took before the flash came, and how lucid and simple it all seems to be now. You will all of you know precisely what I mean if I say the words "dominant seventh". The words present no kind of difficulty to your understanding, and their meaning is so obvious to you now, that it is not easy to believe that once they had a puzzling and oracular mystery about them. The idea conveyed by the words is itself pellucidly simple, and your only real difficulty was in arriving at the idea through the words in which it had to be expressed. So when you have to teach such things to your pupils always remember that the difficulty does not lie in the idea, but in their arriving at flashpoint from the things you say.

Objective Explanation. In its early stages all explanation is objective; that is to say, you teach the name of the thing in question, or else illustrate the thing from its name. If a child asks you what an angle is, you explain—and probably draw an example of—two straight lines meeting. If a beginner points to the odd-looking symbol at the beginning of a piece of music and asks what it is, you tell him it is a clef. The only real danger in this early stage is that of telling too much, often from a conscientious desire to tell the whole truth. It is true that, from your example of an angle, the child may henceforth think of it as a "corner"; but he will not suffer seriously from that limitation, since, until he learns Trigonometry, there is no necessity for him to know that you also get an angle by going round the other way. And I have known a "thorough" music-mistress so thrilled at a child volunteering a question about a clef that she straightway enumerated all the clefs there are; and it is difficult to think of any information less likely to stimulate a beginner.

Explanation of a primary kind, such as the above examples typify, is little more than imparting information; an important matter, if only for the purpose of increasing vocabulary. But a little further on we find ourselves called on to use comparison and analogy, and here comes in the precept, familiar to all of you, that our explanation must be *from the known to the unknown.* "What is a Gorilla?" brings the answer "a very large monkey, as big as a man, and stronger". A 'cello is "a large violin which plays the bass, and is much too large to go under the chin". A Cathedral is an enormous church, Cavalry means soldiers on horseback, and if you asked me what kind of a game baseball is I should say at once "Did you ever play Rounders?" The method is so natural and usual that you will hear with some surprise that logicians dignify it with the name of "Definition *per genus et differentiam*". You name the family group, and specify the individual difference.

Subjective Explanation. Objective explanation is clearly right in the early stages of any subject. But there comes a time in the education of the mind when the crucial condition of understanding a thing is the apprehension of the idea or principle lying behind some abstract words and mental progress depends on grasping it. And in such cases the inexperienced, or unaccomplished, or lazy teacher is apt to fall back on objective in place of the more difficult subjective explanation. For instance, when asked what the word "Courage" means, such a teacher is tempted to tell a story of some man or woman's brave action, adding "It was Courage that enabled him to do that". An even lazier teacher might say that Courage meant "feeling no fear". Even with the young such definitions are dangerous, and may be positively harmful; for every child knows that he experiences fear, and might despondently assume that he never could be brave. Men who have done really brave things can seldom be induced to talk about them, but of those whom I have listened to all agreed on one point: that they were "frightened out of their lives" the whole time. The true definition of Courage, and the most important aspect of it educationally, is that it is the power of inhibiting fear.

There are many words in the Art of Music which are difficult to apprehend and even more difficult to explain; but no one can acquire musicianship without assimilating the inner meaning of such words, so that, even if you are never going to teach, it will be good for you to apply your minds to a few of them, as it is more than likely that in some cases the "flash of intuition" has, up to the present, passed you by.

(1) *Key*. This is a word you will frequently be called upon to explain. Do not take refuge in saying that there is one flat in the key of F, and that if you find two flats then the key is B flat, and so on. That is objective explanation. What your pupils have to realize, if they are to be musicians, is that "key" does not mean a scale, or a particular collection of notes, but that our minds have a curious and ineradicable habit of co-ordinating notes to a Tonic. Young pianists always tend to think of a key as so many white notes and so many black: young violinists think in terms of the position of the left hand; to singers, young and old, it is just a matter of notation. If once you see that it is none of these things in essence, then you may well spend a little time in thinking over how you are going to explain it.

(2) *Intervals*. It has often happened to me, in my supervision of teachers, that I have come into a room when a class was being introduced to Intervals. The procedure has been almost invariably the same. The teacher writes on the blackboard various two-note chords, and explains that one is called a major third, one a minor sixth, and so on. Now this method is, psychologically, definitely wrong, and that for a very simple reason: it is trying to teach two things at a time. An interval, such as the two just named, is always expressed as a number (if for the moment we allow "unison" and "octave" to represent numbers) with an adjective in front of it; two entirely distinct ideas, arrived at by equally distinct methods.

Quite small children can be made absolutely safe in arriving at the number, since it only involves counting out seven letters of the alphabet on their fingers. But the adjective can only be arrived at securely by knowing the notes of the scale if we use the lower note as Tonic; and small children are not familiar with all the scales. I wonder if all of you, trained musicians as you are, can tell me instantaneouly and with certainty the name of this interval:

Small children might well know enough to say "a sixth"; but few of them would know that in B major the sixth note is G sharp, and that therefore the interval, being one semitone larger, must be an augmented sixth. You may think it is rather an outlandish one to ask, but it is not; its key is D sharp minor, which is the relative minor of F sharp major, and it might, and does, occur in many pieces in five, six, or seven sharps.

To impress you with the importance of this point, try this experiment on your musical friends: put down these two notes on the piano

and ask them what the interval is called. Nine out of ten will at once say "a major third". The tenth, I hope, will be wise enough to ask you the names of the notes. If you say "B sharp and E" or "C and F flat" it is a diminished fourth; and there is no law against you calling one B sharp and the other F flat, in which case it is some exotic kind of a fifth: indeed, there is no reason why, if it pleases you, you might not call one D double-flat and the other D double-sharp, when the interval must be called some kind of a nightmare unison.

So keep the number and the adjective quite distinct; teach the number as early as you like, but keep the adjective until your pupils have a working acquaintance with their scales.

(3) *Time.* This is one of those words, already regretted, which we in England use in so many different senses that children's minds are in a fog the moment they hear the word. We speak of "fast and slow time", "simple and compound time", "strict and free time", and, if there is a repeat, "first and second time". So it can do nothing but good to examine the word.

Now we live in a dimension called Time, and in that dimension music has its whole existence, just as architecture has its whole existence in the dimension of Space. But "Musical-Time" is something which results from our treatment of the Time-dimension. If we do nothing to the time in which we live, beyond letting it peacefully flow, then it has no connection with music beyond being a medium in which music *might* exist. If you tap the table, at exactly equal intervals and without accent, you have merely divided a part of the time in which we live into equal sections; again, nothing to do with music. If you tap the table in the same way again, but this time accenting taps 1, 3, 5, etc., *or* taps 1, 4, 7, etc., then you have grouped your taps into systems which may serve as the basis either of "bars" for the composer or "feet" for the poet. You have, as it were, provided a symmetrical trellis-work which may serve as the canvas for words or for musical sounds; and when used for musical sounds it is called "Time". Do it on the piano, on one note, with the accents as before, and you will have provided, in spite of the monotony and absence of feeling, perfect examples of "two in a bar" and "three in a bar"—the only two Times that exist.

The last six words may surprise you; you may at once say "What about four-in-a-bar?" A moment's reflection should convince you that, in any piece of music in Common Time, you can change the time-signature to 2/2 without making any difference to it whatever. Were you not taught that in Common Time there is a strong accent on the first beat of the bar, and a "secondary" accent on the third beat? That is a perfectly frank avowal of the fact that the time is "duple".

The difficulties of teaching Time are entirely due, not to any musical difficulty in the idea, but to the arithmetical complications of Time-signatures. Consider a simple phrase

then consider this

The two phrases are identical in every way except in script. To call one quadruple time and the other duple is merely stating a fact about the script, as unconnected with the essential idea of Time as would be the printing of one example in red ink and the other in blue. For that idea is the one of recurrent accent in groups of two or three, and is nothing else; though there are many charming compositions in which by alternating these groups—2 + 3 or 3 + 2—composers give us works in so-called five-time.

One more point—the perennial difficulty of getting children to apperceive "compound Time". Recently I supervised a class in which the teacher was talking about Time, and to my delight she began with a truth: "There are only two kinds of Time", she said. Then, to my distress, she added "Simple and compound". This is just another case of confusing the arithmetical-basis with the accent-basis. If apples are "three a penny" you cannot go into a shop and buy only one without having a discussion and making some sort of a bargain; the arithmetic of our coinage forbids it. It has nothing whatever to do with the value of the apples or of your money, and if there happened to be a coin worth a third of a penny the transaction would be simple. Similarly, you must often have been asked to put a bass to a melody. Suppose the melody is in 2/4 time, and you arrive at a bar with two crotchets in it. If you choose a minim for your bars, or two crotchets, or four quavers, no problem arises in writing them down; but you may think it would be nice to have three notes in the bass to each crotchet in the tune. Then there must clearly be a "wangle", merely because, like the penny, a crotchet will not divide into three. You have, by the common consent of writers of music, two courses open to you. You can write your three-note groups as "triplets"—

in which case the wangle consists in pretending that there can be three quavers in a crotchet. Or you can wangle by saying "Let's make the beat into a dotted crotchet, and pretend a dotted crotchet can be equal to two quavers ":

But all the above six bars are identical in Time, for 6/8 time would automatically cease to exist if we were sensible enough to invent a note which was a third of a crotchet.

(4) *Rhythm*. This is admittedly a difficult word to apperceive, and still more difficult, as some of you have already discovered, to explain. But it would be less difficult if musicians would ask themselves where it *begins*. Play, quite normally, some tune of exactly equal notes, such as this hymn-tune:

No fault can be found with the Time of this example, nor with its *Metre*—which is the grouping, on some symmetrical plan, of its Tune-accents. But the question of Rhythm has not arisen, and does not arise until there is some deviation from the pure Time-pattern. Many folk think that by accenting more and more the first and third beats of each bar they would be making it more and more rhythmical, whereas they would only be accentuating the Time. You know the way in which children will sometimes say a line of poetry with exaggerated accents on the strong beats. "The *way* was *long*, the *wind* was *cold*." We do not call that rhythm, but "sing-song": and you could not make your minim hymn-tune rhythmical merely by thumping the accents. Many musicians, having themselves acquired a delicate sense of rhythm, will disagree with these statements, or at best think the whole matter purely academic. But since the word is admittedly difficult to explain it is surely best to attempt to find where the difficulty lies; and primarily it will be found to lie in not recognizing that Time provides the normal accent-system, and rhythm is not born until there occurs some deviation from that norm. Any child can grasp that in the "Easter hymn" the first four bars establish a time-norm, while the second four illustrate rhythm:

So before you tackle Rhythm make certain that the Time-sense is secure, and you will then have no trouble in showing that on that adamantine system it is possible to overlay any kind of pattern or arabesque you may choose.

One more point is worth making, for the sake of clearness. You will remember that *Metre* was described as the grouping of bars or feet on some plan. Your minds are so constituted that, in listening to musical phrases you unconsciously (or subconsciously) *count* the accented beats in a phrase, and expect the next phrase to balance. If the organist in church were to play over the hymn-tune as follows:

almost everyone in the congregation would know that something had "gone wrong". For they had subconsciously realized that the first phrase contained four stresses, and their sense of balance asked that the second should have four stresses as well. This is what we are referring to when we speak of *Bar-rhythm*, or *Secondary rhythm*, and it is often an interesting feature in music. Have you ever discovered that the Brahms' "Variations on a Theme of Haydn", and his part-song "Vineta" are both in five-bar rhythm? At the end of the Meistersinger, where the various guild-processions come in one after another there is a witty instance. They come in to tunes which are mostly in normal eight-bar phrases, but now and then a guild, in its eagerness to assert itself, begins before its predecessor has finished, lopping off the last bar so that, if you are not shrewd, you might imagine Wagner had "miscounted". This kind of lopping, or dove-tailing, occurs fairly often in the folksongs which I hope you will teach your classes:

(Billy Boy)

For she is too young to be   tak-en from her mammy,   For she is

Whether such a device was due to a deliberate artistic invention, to a simple miscalculation, or to an undeveloped sense of balance, or merely to a mistake on the part of the singer from whom it was taken down, will, I think, never be determined with certainty.

(5) *Phrasing.* This, again, you will find an extremely difficult word to explain; but since it is the acid-test of musicianship in all performance it is clearly worth thinking about. No words you can use will ever bring the "flash of intuition" to even your cleverest pupil; but there are many facts which a good teacher will bring to notice, and each fact absorbed erects a milestone. Here are four, given in the hope that you will think out a dozen more for yourselves:

(a) Phrasing is punctuation. The necessity of taking breath in speaking has led to the invention of commas, semi-colons, and full-stops, in order that we may provide ourselves with opportunities to breathe. And the mind feels the necessity for the same points of rest. I remember being given an example, as a schoolboy, of how one missing comma may make a sentence contradict itself:

"Always tell the truth—if you can't, tell a good lie". You may think the advice morally doubtful, but you will probably agree that there are occasions when the truth must be suppressed—as in "Am I going to die, Doctor?"—and when an untruth is demanded a bold one is better than a shuffling conscience-salving weakling. But omit the comma, and you have "Always tell the truth—if you can't tell a good lie."

Now the end of a slur in a musical phrase always means at least a comma. You are at that point to take a mental breath, and definitely to cut short the last note and put in a rest, however short. Can you sing, or play, or even think of this phrase without including the three short silences for which the composer asks, by his phrase-marks instead of by rests?

(b) Normally, the highest note is the climax, and tonally the most important. This is for the physical reason that extra height in pitch means extra tension in vocal-cords; and the mind has in consequence become habituated to coupling the higher note with the greater emotional stress. The least important beat in Common Time is the fourth in the bar; yet to which note would any of you intuitively give the greatest importance in the following?

(c) A long slur is often merely a general instruction to play smoothly. But short slurs often tell you quite definitely that the accent is to be redistributed, and the rests to be inserted in different places. You will probably agree that the following phrase is reasonably interpreted:

played

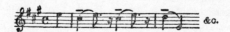

but the phrase happens, in the original, to be set out as:

and I think you would want to play it as:

(d) Tied notes are often interpreted by children as meaning merely that you need not take the trouble to strike the key again. Most of them—and many grown-ups—never realize that when a composer ties a note on a weak beat to one on a strong beat he is asking you to transfer to the weak beat, by a kind of syncopation, accent belonging to the strong one. In the following example, I think you will all agree that the least important of all the seven notes is the third: it needs only the slightest tap, just to keep the movement going:

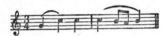

But if the composer ties the third and fourth notes, does it not become the most important of the seven?

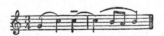

There are many other things you will wish your pupils to understand, and your talks and explanations will guide them along the track to the promised land. The only golden rule is invariably to connect any explanation with an illustration of it in sound. In teaching Cadences, for example, it is of little real use to tell a pupil that an "Amen" is a plagal cadence; it might just as well be a half-close in another key. But they all know "Good King Wenceslas", and realize that its final cadence is out of the ordinary. If you should ever talk to them about Modes, do not give them mere statistical information about the Mixo-Lydian or Hypo-Ionian, etc.; that is only knowledge from the outside. Make them sing "Searching for

lambs" or "What shall we do with a drunken sailor?" and the real
tang and taste of the Modes will be theirs for life. The intelligent
pupils, again, may even ask you why a chord ugly in itself is ever used;
and the answer is the purely psychological one that relief is the most
exquisite form of pleasure—as you find out when your toothache
stops. If you were given these three notes as bass, tenor, and alto
and were asked to put in the treble

would it ever occur to you to write F sharp? Try the four notes,
and shudder at their ugliness. Then play:

Again, play this chord

which I am sure you will admit to be ugly. Then play the opening of

"Annie Laurie" and see if there is any other chord could take its
place.

   You have often heard that dirt is "matter in the wrong place".
It is equally true that beauty is frequently ugliness in the right one.

There are two Methods which are genuinely helpful when we want to get at the ideas lying behind facts.

(1) *The Genetic Method.* Genesis means "origin", and the Genetic Method pays tribute to the fact that if you desire to comprehend anything properly you must trace out how it came to be what it is. There is nothing "highbrow" about this. Can you not recall someone you know whose character was, for a time, a puzzle to you? You could not anticipate their reactions, nor find a satisfactory solution for their way of looking at things. Then you get a chance of greater intimacy; you stay with her and see her home life and environment, or you meet her parents and see the kind of opinions and character that have influenced her formative years. All of a sudden you find the "key", and feel that under the same circumstances your own outlook on life would probably have been very similar to hers. Again, if you had to "get up" the English Constitution for an examination, you would find yourself very ill-equipped if you had confined yourself to studying what it is at the present day, for it is past comprehension to anyone who has not tried to trace its origin and gradual growth.

In music the Genetic Method is a plea, and a very powerful one, for the study of History, both musical and civil; for without any knowledge of history a deep understanding of music is impossible. A knowledge of the later medieval Church, however slight, will fertilize your understanding of Byrd and Palestrina; a knowledge of the Reformation period, even a superficial one, will immensely increase your interest in Bach; without some glimmering of what the word Renaissance stands for you will miss being in at the very birth of modern music; and without any idea of what the Romantic Movement implied you must miss, however much you enjoy the music of Beethoven and Chopin, all understanding of the dynamic impulses which brought them forth and sustained them.

(2) The second is called the *Historical Method.* It means that, if you would appraise anything arising from another period, you must put yourself in the shoes of a contemporary.

You and I are perhaps a little surprised at the way in which Henry VIII treated his wives; but to the people of his time—even the ecclesiastics—it did not seem specially abnormal, and those who did deprecate it would have given reasons very different from yours and mine. If we apply Bond-street standards of dress to the ladies of Polynesia we are only stultifying ourselves.

You will not then grasp the aims of any composer who lived before your own period unless you can imagine yourself as a contemporary member of his audience; forgetting for the moment all that music has done since in providing more sophisticated ways of expressing emotion. Those who have never learned to transplant themselves in this way, forgetting that every style, however archaic it now seems, was once modern, are apt to think that the older composers had no emotion to express. But once discover how to eliminate the intervening centuries and to take your seat in their audience as a contemporary, and you will find that their power over the material and the ways and means open to them was so astonishing that we ourselves, accomplishing so much less with such ampler opportunities, may well be filled with admiration and humility.

CHAPTER ELEVEN

APPRECIATION

THE most important change that has happened in the last fifty years, in regard to the teaching of music, is undoubtedly due to the recognition of one fact: that whereas in the old days "learning music" meant solely being taught to play or sing, it nowadays includes, as a matter of at least equal importance, learning to recognize and understand good music.

In those days, if you wished to prove how good a teacher you were, you had but one thing to do. You gathered your pupils together and made them play, then asked the listeners to pronounce that it was good playing. Nowadays any good judge of your work would question the pupils as to their sensitiveness towards the music. The means by which this change of attitude has come about is now usually called the teaching of Appreciation; and though many musicians dislike the word, and suspect that it too often means just cramming a child with undigested jargon about First-movement Form, yet it is difficult to find a better label, and in the right hands, using intelligent methods, valuable results can certainly be obtained.

My object now is not to give you a précis of useful talks which you may hereafter deliver to your classes, since, if your teaching is to bear fruit, it must originate in your own mind and experience: that is, from what your own mind has found out and assimilated from the experience of your own growth in discrimination. I shall attempt only to make you think, a little below the surface, as to what the word Appreciation means.

The first important fact is this. Words beginning with AP, you will find, generally imply the suggestion of "Valuation". To "praise" a thing has a simple meaning; to "appraise" it means to bring it before some tribunal of your mind, and to estimate its worth. To "prove" conveys a simple idea; to "approve" is to say that you have applied some standard of judgment which the object has satisfied. This rather obvious point is worth insisting on because once, at an international meeting on Appreciation, a speaker (who had travelled from a far country) rose up and threw cold water on "philosophical nonsense", saying, with all the assurance of a closed mind, "If I really like anything, then I appreciate it". He should have been told, but was not, that the simple fact that so many people "really like" bad music is the whole *raison d'être* of a discussion on Appreciation.

Works of Art are, as you will all agree, works of Imagination. So let us first get a clear idea of what we mean by that word.

The best definition of Imagination that I know is one which will probably surprise you. It is not "fancy", or "day-dreaming", or "building castles in the air", but "the power of seeing things as they really are". Perhaps an illustration will convince you. Have you not, amongst your friends or those you admire, someone whom you knew, possibly for a considerable time, before discovering their value? You put them down as self-centred, unimaginative, or dull; them something happened which enlightened you as to their true character and you saw how woefully mistaken your estimate had been. You had not had enough imagination to see the gold beneath the surface.

Imagination is of two kinds; these used to be called *Creative* and *Receptive*, but are now more generally labelled *Productive* and *Reproductive*.

(a) *Productive, or Creative Imagination* is constructive, and it is abstract in character. The artist who feels, and can translate his feeling into words, paint, or musical notes, is constructive and has Creative Imagination. It is not common, as you know, in its higher forms, because the ability to get feeling into form implies technique, and people gifted with imagination are often too impatient to master the methods of expressing it; which is one reason for the phrase "mute, inglorious Miltons".

(b) *Reproductive Imagination* is reconstructive; concrete and particular. All children possess it, as you discover if you tell them a story. Tell them that same story a second time, and woe betide you if the princess' gown is blue when the previous time it had been red. They visualize the story, and see mental-images of your castles and dragons.

Appreciation is the application to anything of the Receptive Imagination. Beethoven feels, and enshrines his feelings in a Waldstein Sonata. You play the notes printed, and you may "like" the result; but it is not till you have recaptured the feeling which urged him to compose the work, or think that you have, that you have any right to say you appreciate it. You have then penetrated below the surface, and your imagination has reconstructed his emotional purpose.

There is one special danger, so persistent and so surreptitious that you should always be on your guard against it, for it is the enemy of all criticism. It is that we often think we appreciate a thing when our enjoyment and approval are really due to some secondary cause; or, *per contra*, some secondary reason strangles an appreciation which should be there. Can you be quite sure of giving a just judgment on a performance, independently of whether the performer is a person you are devoted to, or loathe? There is a useful word to add to your vocabulary in this connection: *quâ*, meaning "as an example of". Imagine a man who has never tasted tea. If he were tortured with thirst and you poured out a cup for him, he might well say "What a delicious cup of tea"; but he is appreciating it *quâ* drink, not *quâ* tea. So you, on hearing your first fugue, might say "what a perfect fugue"; but you would be judging it *quâ* music—for all you know it may, *quâ* fugue, be but a poor specimen. Many a "thriller" is all that we could ask of it, *quâ* thriller; but do not tell your friends it is a "fine book", for that would imply excellence *quâ* literature.

Appreciation passes through three main stages, and so it can be roughly divided into three classes: *crude, intelligent,* and *critical.*

Crude appreciation. Someone, possibly a relation of the gentleman at the International Congress, once said "If I could appreciate anything as a dog appreciates a bone, I should be satisfied".

Now a dog's appreciation of a bone depends on two things: (1) Is it his first bone? If so he may appreciate it *quâ* food, but not *quâ* bone. (2) If it is not his first bone, can he recall the others for purposes of comparison? Crude appreciation is sensational: i.e. in our first experience of anything we can only say we like or dislike. The cat, feeling the warmth of the fire for the first time in its life, enjoys it as an alternative to the cold outside. On the second occasion he has a rudimentary standard of judgment, and is entitled to say "This is a better fire than last night's". And at this point he has entered on the stage of

Intelligent Appreciation. This involves judgment, at first elementary, but growing in breadth and value as our apperception-masses are enlarged. We have an ever-increasing bundle of experiences of things, not as a rule formulated into any system of valuation, but sufficiently realized to enable us to give a verdict, and possibly to justify it. As these systems of valuation become more and more developed they gradually become for us our principles of judgment, and we are then approaching to

Critical Appreciation. When you have acquired the feeling of "security of judgment" you have no further to go. You may be right or wrong in your verdicts: that depends on the calibre of your mind. But you will know that your verdicts of good or bad are not founded on personal caprice, since you have built up an apparatus of discrimination; and you will know that your private likings and dislikings have not been allowed to over-ride your judgment. We speak of certain people "having good taste" as if it were a gift from heaven; but few, if any, of us are born liking the best things. Is it reasonable to suppose that the great minds of the world of Art—the Shakespeares, the Bachs, the Michael Angelos —the men who have penetrated deepest into life's mysteries, will embody their thoughts and feelings in ways that can be apprehended by an untutored child?

Although care has been taken to point out that "liking" does not constitute appreciation, it is nevertheless necessary that appreciation should include liking. It would be a little disingenuous and absurd to say "I do appreciate that sonata, but I don't like it". It is not until you have learnt to love the things which your judgment tells you are fine, and to loathe those you judge to be bad, that you have truly reached the stage of critical appreciation. For it involves both Feeling and Understanding, which is why it has been defined as "realization of value, plus appeal".

As teachers your business will be to raise all of your pupils from the crude to the intelligent class, and as many as you can from the intelligent to the critical stage; and my own experience is that a large percentage of human beings can be brought, with patience and guidance, if not to an undisputed position in the critical class, at least so far on the road to it as to be at all events in sight of the promised land.

There are three *Caveats* I should like to set before you, and it may stretch your minds, and help them to stray down some side-avenues of thought, if you will consider them.

Caveat I. Do not allow critical acumen to deaden your emotional reactions. It is too often the case that the expert confines his attention to technique. Go to the theatre with an actor-friend, and you will be astonished at how little of his attention has been given to the play; you may even find he is surprised that you think it of such importance. Once I found myself with a painter, looking at a charming picture of a child with her hands behind her back. He simply refused to consider it, saying, with some contempt, that the artist had evaded the difficulty of painting the hands. And in the early days of Wagner—I mean the days when we in England were rather tentatively making acquaintance with his works—a musician of importance at the time refused either to listen to or discuss the Meistersinger Prelude on the ground that, according to him, the second subject was in the same key as the first; whilst an eminent critic pronounced Tchaikovsky's Fifth Symphony to be no symphony at all, because it had a waltz in it.

Caveat II. Remember that we do not, and cannot, "understand" Art, for the reason that the part we understand is not Art. Yet Art *must* reach the Feelings viâ the Understanding. This is a great philosophical truth, fundamental to all musical appreciation, and is not nearly so cryptic as it sounds. To repeat an example you have had before, were I to say to you, on a late November evening, "It is getting dark quickly now", I am making a plain conversational statement of fact, with no Art about it. When the poet says "Fast falls the eventide" he is making precisely the same statement as I did, but is calling in the art of poetry in order, somehow or other, to touch your emotions. If he had said it, even more poetically, in Chinese, you would have had no artistic reaction (except, maybe, to the beauty of the mere sound of voice or words) simply because you did not understand. Were you to say "that is a beautiful picture, but I cannot tell you whether it is a sunset or a house on fire" you are clearly talking nonsense; though, again, you may like it *quâ* a splash of colour. Before it can reach your feelings you must understand it; after that you can apply to it your powers of critical appreciation.

Caveat III. It is a common remark that an Artist constructs a work of Imagination; a statement which, though true, is only half true. Out of his own imagination he has created his work; but his real object is to make you and me, by the use of *our* imagination, reconstruct it; and his success or failure in doing this is the great critical criterion. It is possible that you have, at the end of a novel, found yourself with a lump in your throat and tears running down your cheeks—although you knew perfectly well that you had been reading about events which never happened and people who never lived. The novelist did, of course, construct the work of imagination you have been reading, but the proof of his success lay in the fact that he made you reconstruct it all with such actuality that, for the time being, it was the world in which you were living. If you had finished your reading entirely unmoved his object, in your particular case, would have been unattained, whether from want of skill on his part, or want of receptivity on yours. And if you see that all Art is an attack by one man's skill on another's receptivity, and think of the varying degrees of receptivity of your own friends and relations, then you will realize how far criticism must always be from an exact science.

So in music a composer may say that his work is created solely to get into shape some emotional stress—that is, to relieve his feelings—or to "project his personality". But if his music does not touch any of us, then he has failed to make us, through our reconstructive imagina-

G

tions, recognize what his emotions were—that is, we cannot see why he wrote it.

The appreciation of all great music calls for a recognition of this combination of feeling and understanding, and allowing for differences of balance in different composers. There is plenty to "understand" in a Chopin Ballade, and plenty to "feel" in a Bach Fugue; but the ratio is different.

Fifty years ago people, even musical people, were given to saying that there was no feeling to be found in Bach, or that it was mere bragging to pretend to understand Brahms. So if ever you find yourself unable to make sense of, or feel moved by, music (or anything else) which is new and strange do not be quick to condemn. For it may merely be that, for the time being, the lens of your mind has not learned to focus on the new object, and that your growth and expansion, both in Understanding and Appreciation, depend on the effort you make in readjusting your mind and increasing your receptivity.

CHAPTER TWELVE

WILL

THE field of Psychology is a large one; it might, indeed, be called limitless, since its principles and truths can be adapted and applied to any subject as easily as to Music. But when we have explored all its avenues, however superficially, we are inevitably confronted with the fact that, if our discoveries are to be of any practical value to ourselves or others, one further thing is required: the Will to act upon them. We can *learn* from Psychology things which will so systematize our outlook that every thought and action should be logical, considered, and fertile. But all we have learnt will be sterile and valueless unless it be put into practice by the power of the Will. It may help us, therefore, to make some inquiries as to what this mysterious power is.

The English, for a "practical" race—accustomed to making up their minds (even too quickly) and acting, and given to a slight contempt for the "theorizers" who urge reflection—are curiously enigmatic in their use of words connected with will-power. Any Englishman will claim to admire "determination"; but when it is displayed by an antagonist he labels it "obstinacy". "Desire" has acquired a connection with sex which renders its use more than a little dangerous. "Wish" has become almost a word suggesting the impossible: you wish the rain would stop, or that you had never been born. "Voluntary" is almost a negation of all the compelling qualities which will-power implies; for if you were told that your attendance at these lectures was voluntary, you would understand that you need not settle any course, but just come or not as you liked at the moment. So psychologists use the word "volition", which the dictionary tells us means "Exercise of the Will, or the power of Willing".

At first sight you might perhaps think that matters of Will fell rather into the domain of Ethics, or even of Philosophy, rather than Psychology. But you will at once trace the connection when you consider the psychological maxim that *All Will ends in Action.* Students are sometimes foolish enough to learn such aphorisms by heart, for examination purposes, without ever realizing their simple and practical implications. If you happen to be reading, late at night, and on hearing the clock strike midnight you say to yourself "I am determined to go to bed", you have merely formed a resolution. To exercise your Will you must shut up the book and get out of the armchair. The question now arises as to whether all actions, or which kind of actions, involve the use of Will; and psychologists divide actions into three classes:

(a) *Reflex Actions.* These are altogether outside the scope of the Will, and can only be connected with it by an act of Inhibition. Let me recall the simple instance I gave you in an earlier lecture. If anything touches your eyelashes, you blink; that is a reflex action, a provision of Nature for the protection of your eyes. But if I tell you I am going to make you blink by touching them you could possibly, by exercising will-power, inhibit the reaction; though if a speck of dust were to touch them unawares the next moment, the reaction will assuredly occur.

(b) *Voluntary Actions.* Our first infantile actions, such as snatching or crying, are all involuntary, many of them being purely instinctive; some indeed—such as blushing—remain involuntary all our lives, often to our regret, and have more than a little in common with reflexes. They are due to a stimulus, and through being exercised the reactions grow into habits. In given cases we rehearse mentally the action we are going to take, without considering alternatives. You want to brush away a fly which is irritating your forehead, so one of your hands moves up to perform the action, your mind rehearsing its movements in advance. This "mental rehearsal", though it may sound merely doctrinaire, is a very real thing, and is of considerable importance to musicians. If you ask a pianist to play such a chord as

the mere act of looking at it sets nerves and muscles on a hair-trigger, ready to "explode in action" at the right moment. Look at that chord again, then suddenly look at this one

I feel certain that—at all events in the case of those of you who are pianists—you have actually felt a "switch" in the muscles of your hand, and are now prepared, should you be asked to play the chord, for a different set of muscular actions. That is "mental rehearsal", and it occurs in every voluntary action we make; with the old proviso that when the action has become automatic a nerve-centre will relieve the brain of the duty of supervision.

I have previously pointed out to you how in "reading"—whether "outloud" from a book, or printed music—we are always looking at a word or a chord well ahead of the one we are pronouncing or playing. Your mind has "rehearsed" the necessary movements for fingers or tongue; and the distance between the chord you are playing and the one you are looking at is an index of your power of muscular-memory and your skill as a sight-reader.

Voluntary actions, involving no choice, are sometimes labelled *Ideo-motor*, which means that some idea—such as the percept of the above chords—has created a motor impulse. And the obvious fact that the action is always subsequent to its mental rehearsal is important, because technical progress depends almost entirely on reducing the gap between them to a minimum. If I hold out my pencil in my hand, and ask you to keep your eye on it, you can; if I then move my hand in a circle you can still keep your eye on the pencil. But if suddenly I make my circle in the reverse direction you lose sight of the pencil for a moment, because you have "prepared" your eyes to move in a certain circular path, and have not had time to re-adjust and issue new orders. That is the fact on which all conjuring has to rely. Again, you and I can glance at a series of letters—say WOLVERHAMPTON—and "take in" the word so rapidly that the process seems to be practically instantaneous; but have you not sometimes passed through a station in a fast train, seen the letters of its name, but found yourself unable to piece them together into a word?

You will remember that stress has been laid, in earlier chapters, on the fact that the satisfactory performance of a complex action involves mastering each separate movement before combining them; how learning to waltz means mastering certain steps until suddenly the combination of movements fuses into a whole. That is also the only way of salvation in acquiring the more recondite accomplishments of the musician. Most of you, I feel sure, would like to be able to transpose; and may be surprised to hear that you can do it now, though with a time-lag that makes your attempts of no practical value. If you exercise your will, and resolve to practise, the one and only thing you have to do is to reduce the time that it takes you to look at a chord in one key and see what it would be in another. With yourselves, as with your pupils, you should begin with something easy enough to be encouraging. Take some such example as this:

You can all of you "feel" your fingers on the first chord. How many seconds does it take you to "feel" the same chord in the key of B flat? Even if you have to take ten seconds you would find that, with a very little practice, you could reduce it to eight, then six, then four, and so on. My faith in the human brain forbids me to believe that any one of you could not, with five minutes practice a day, reach in a month the stage when you could play quite easily the first three chords of any hymn tune in any key named. If you could, you have passed the *pons asinorum*, and further excellence in transposition depends henceforth on nothing but your own resolve.

Similarly you could learn to read from score, however bad you may prove at first, by taking an easy partsong, or the adagio of a string-quartet, and begin by playing only the treble and the bass— to widen the "stretch of the eye" that has probably been confined to two-stave piano music. Then add one inner part, and later both. Spend as long as you like over each chord, for every experiment is reducing your time-lag; and in the end you will discover, if you have ambition and perseverance, that even a full score is not so insurmountably difficult as it may seem to you now.

(c) *Determined Actions*. The suggestion for the idea which leads to action may be either *external* or *internal*. You may go into a room, see a tumbler and a jug of lemonade and help yourself to a drink; or see a piano and sit down and "try" it. The immediate cause of your action was not thirst, or love of music, but the chance sight of certain external things which "put the idea in your head". Or you may be assiduously practising when suddenly you remember that to-morrow is your mother's birthday, and you haven't written the letter. And I hope such an internal idea would lead to action.

Now there arises a piece of close psychological reasoning which is sometimes found a little difficult.

Determined Action is always due to a *Motive*; and a Motive is due to an Internal Idea *plus* Feeling. You want to improve; that internal idea suggests to you that you should get up and practise before breakfast. But whether you actually do so or not depends on how strongly you desire to improve—i.e. on whether the strength of your desire is sufficient to make you put the idea into practice. This is sometimes expressed by saying that "Strength of Feeling governs persistence of Motive"; the strength of your thirst governs your persistency in finding something to drink.

Of these two factors in Motive—Idea and Feeling—the Idea is a "constant" whereas the Feeling is a "variable". This sounds rather academic and forbidding, but its meaning is simple. The idea which led you to form a resolution on New Year's Day is exactly the same idea when February arrives, but the feeling about it, which was so strong and urgent at the rather emotional moment of its birth, has generally so vapourized that you find yourself wondering how you ever came to be so sentimental as to register the vow.

This is the point where, not only in New Year resolutions but in everything in life, Will comes into play. Feeling has faded away, as it always will, and can no longer maintain the supremacy of the *ego* over the *me*. There is nothing in the world you can call to your aid except Will; and if you have not kept that in working order, by constant reliance on it in all the small matters of life, woe betide you in the crises.

It is easy to see that here Psychology approaches the domain of Ethics and Morality—two subjects on which it is no part of my duty to preach to you. It is, however, so easy and so usual to assert that a knowledge of the processes of the Mind can have no bearing on Art or on Character, that I hope you will not think it officious or sententious of me to point out that, if you desire to be an asset to the world you live in, a testimonial to the Institution that has tried to train you, and a human being who has any right to indulge in self-respect, then your end will only be attained by the inflexibility with which you master and exercise your will-power.

CHAPTER THIRTEEN

THE MEANING OF EDUCATION

SHOULD some inquisitive questioner, such as Socrates, come and ask you whether, when you have children of your own, you intend to have them educated, you would, I imagine, with one accord answer, Yes. If he then, after his manner, were to ask you Why? it would be extremely interesting to hear your replies.

If this Education is such a desirable and precious thing that you will on no account withhold it from your children, you surely must be quite clear as to what you mean by the word. If, however, you find you are at all vague about its connotation it should be worth while to probe a little into the subject, since its main principles are as necessary in, and as applicable to, the teaching of Music as to any other form of improving our mental grip and grasp of things.

When a philosopher—which means anyone who "thinks"—is confronted with a problem he asks himself three questions about it; and each question can be epitomized in a monosyllable: What, Why, and How. I hope that you were taught at school to think out your essays on those lines. Suppose you had to write an essay on Sport you are not intended to enumerate all the games you know. You should begin by inquiring "What is Sport?" It is obviously, for instance, something quite different from a game, since Chess is a game but not a sport, and pheasant-shooting a sport but not a game. "Why" do you have it in life: what is its end and purpose, and is it desirable or undesirable? If the former, "How" are you going to promote it? Surely the worst essay-writer amongst you could, for a few pages, clothe that skeleton? Next time you have an unoccupied evening try to outline, in some such way, the precis of an essay on "What is Art"; and even if your paper never attains the dignity of being delivered as a lecture, it will have taken you on to another milestone on the road of clear thinking.

What then, do we mean by the word Education?

The first point to consider—and probably the most important, as it is the most frequently ignored—is this. Education consists of two distinct things: Knowledge and Understanding. They might be labelled Learning and Apperception, or even, in their widest sense, Science and Philosophy. Thinkers discovered, ages ago, that some things are matters of fact, verifiable by reference to standards of measurement. If you say that one log is twice the weight of another, or one stick twice the length, the truth of your statement can be tested, for the things in question are measureable. And all such knowledge falls into the domain of Science.

The same thinkers saw clearly that there were other matters in which no yard-stick could be applied. They had no doubt whatever that one thing could be more beautiful than another, or one man more wicked than his neighbour. But it was plainly nonsense to say that one thing was exactly twice as beautiful as another, or that the saint was just seven times as good as the sinner. And all these immeasurable and imponderable matters fall into the domain of Philosophy.

It is a common mistake to imagine that the Philsopher aims at providing standards of measurement; he knows full well that such a purpose would be unattainable. His aim is to help you and me to think below the surface in the elusive matters with which he deals, until by the grace of heaven, we acquire a certain competence to judge—not authoritatively or infallibly, but always by taking thought—between the good and the bad, the genuine thing and the imitation.

And it is here that a fact emerges which is of quite supreme importance, though presumably unknown—since it is never even mentioned—to the busybodies who write to the papers about Education, or the officials who administer it. And the fact is this. Although the subjects falling into the category of Science are of the very greatest consequence to the human race—for without them we should never have learnt how to build a house or to navigate the seas—yet it is in the category of Philosophy that we find all the matters about which men feel deeply. It is Politics, Art, and Religion that stir men's hearts and tempers. The great minds of the world have thought persistently on these things, opening many avenues and warning us of many pitfalls. But their insight cannot be tabulated into the clearcut systems which the "practical man" can comprehend, so he dismisses them with the shrug of the shoulder which says "everything of that sort is just theorizing". The difference between good and bad, whether in morals, in music, or in anything else, is the one thing in the world which is of vital importance to everyone. And the fact that, when we try to discover that difference, we find the sea uncharted makes its exploration only the more imperative, and points out to us quite unmistakably what we should make the aim of Education.

The unthinking people of the world, those who imagine that the end of Education is information, have always been the drag on its wheels. It should, in their opinion, be exclusively utilitarian, preparing a man for the career he is to follow. "Why on earth should my son learn Trigonometry?" such a man once said. "He is going to be a grocer, so confine his education to the subjects that will help him." There is, unfortunately, a comfortable feeling abroad that such an ignorant point of view has no influence nowadays; but it is difficult to avoid feeling that even our august educational authorities, with their "vocational training", are capitulating to the same heresy under a prettier name.

Information, it may readily be granted, must be the foundation of all education; but not its end and aim. There is, I think, an almost perfect analogy in food. We need health and strength, so we eat and drink; but food is not in itself "health and strength", for these depend on what our digestion does with our food. We need education, and so we acquire information; but our education depends on what our Intellect—which is our mental digestion—does with the information provided. If you are very patient, and have a very good parrot, you might teach it to repeat all the dates in history; but you cannot make a parrot into a historian, simply because you cannot educate him.

The Greek philosophers pointed out that a man has four sides to his nature, these four sides, as it were plaited together, constituting the whole man. They form four categories, and every human activity can find its place in one or other of them. These four sides are:

(1) *Physical*—dealing with the body
(2) *Intellectual*—dealing with thought
(3) *Aesthetic*—dealing with the feelings
(4) *Moral*—dealing with conduct and character

To the Greeks education meant training and control in all these four divisions; and though the idea may at first seem far-fetched it is worth considering whether a return to it might not help to solve some of the world's present problems. Certainly the departure from this conception of Education is responsible for a great part of the antagonism in national ideals from which our troubles now arise. In my own student days, for instance, it is not far wide of the mark to say that German education centred round (2) and (3), almost to the exclusion of (1) and (4); whereas in England (1) and (4) were all-important, (2) very subsidiary, and (3) completely ignored. Every German I ever knew was only too ready to boast of his country's intellectual and artistic pre-eminence, and if he himself did not happen to be learned or artistic would apologize for the fact with genuine regret. But physical fitness and moral character—though of course both were often met with—were matters of chance.

In England, on the other hand, any Headmaster would claim with pride that, though his boys were perhaps not up to any very high intellectual standard yet they had acquired character and were fine physical specimens. The boys themselves, with a polite assumption of an apologetic tone, might disclaim being "musical" or "brainy", but one could almost hear the sotto-voce "Thank heaven".

It would have seemed odd to the German that the Greek, if a man was getting too obese for his waistcoat, would have called him uneducated; and I should very much like to be there if an English boy, in the next world, were to tell Plato that he thought music was "rather rot". So let us hope that, amongst the many who seem to have strong views about the new education that is to come after the war, and who, from their position in Church and State will be given an opportunity of airing them, there will be one or two of sufficient insight to dismount from their private hobby-horse, and to put the case for the complete man.

To you and me, as musicians, there is a special interest in the third strand—the Aesthetic side—since it is the one round which the main business of our lives is entwined. One of our claims is that Art should take its place in the education of every child: that is to say that all children should grow up in an environment in which care is taken to surround them with beautiful things. It ought not even to be too much to hope that some day a school-building will have been evolved which is not definitely offensive to the eye. In many schools, including the Elementary ones, really beautiful pictures cover the walls, in many really good music is sung, and often sung beautifully. But there is as yet no recognition, official or private, of the fact that the purpose of Education is not to make us learned, but to enable us to discriminate between good and bad, and that if we lack this discrimination in artistic things we shall miss half the joy of life. No man would say that he cares not a rap whether his own children read good or bad books, like good or bad music, have good or bad pictures hung in their nurseries; he wishes them to have their discriminating powers educated. But he is indifferent to the fate of other people's children, thinking, presumably that their imaginations will grow without being fed. He can hardly maintain seriously that if a child's formative years are spent assimilating bad standards no irremediable harm has been done. Children can and do love the very best—witness the popularity of the "Unfinished Symphony". And in my time as Music Adviser to the L.C.C. I discovered, to my surprise and delight, that when asked to choose the most perfect piece of music they had ever heard, many Elementary Schools in London chose Bach's "Jesu, joy of man's desiring".

The real aim of those who teach any branch of Art should be, not merely to produce a select few who will paint or play better because of our teaching, but to awaken and stir the imagination of the whole body; that is our only true justification for pleading for Art in Education. You and I know that the richness or aridity of our lives is conditioned by our Imaginations, but few people realize its full potentiality. Make a list, one day, of the men and women of History to whom you would grant the epithet "great". Plato and Socrates, King Alfred and Napoleon, Florence Nightingale, Darwin, Newton: add or subtract as you choose, you will find but one quality common to all of them. Some were good, some bad; some had great intellectual power, some small; but every one on any possible list will have had "vision". They worked on the same material that was at everyone's disposal, and their imagination transmuted it.

How then, you may ask, is the Imagination to be trained? Games are there for training the body; schoolwork is intended to train the intellect; religion works in the moral field. What means are there for developing and training this great quality of Imagination, without which bare facts can never cluster round a dream? The only method which human wit has ever devised for such a purpose is Art. Many men have been born strong in body, some with fine intellects, a reasonable number with fine character; but only one here and there with real imagination. Those of us who are "just average", but want to reach a little nearer to our ideals, know that only by training—including self-training—shall we fulfil our desire. Why pretend that it is only on our imaginative side that the attempt is not worth making?

The endeavour to educate people who already love music so that they will want that music to be good, may seem at first sight a trivial contribution to make to the world's welfare. So I would like you to meditate on the considered utterances of two fine minds. Ruskin, when questioned on this very point—the influence of Taste on Character—replied: "Tell me the things a man likes, and I will tell you the kind of man he is." And in our own time Professor Mackail, in words you might well frame and hang up as a text, said "To have loved the best, and to have known it for the best, is to have been successful in life".

CHAPTER FOURTEEN

THE ELEMENTS OF THINKING

THE word "thinking", in its primary sense, means exercising the mind, not necessarily with any purpose or interest. To that extent it is an activity which, presumably, we share with the animal world; for your dog must be thinking when he recognizes your voice, since memory is a function of the mind. "The mind is always attending to something" is an acknowledgement of the fact that we are thinking throughout our conscious life. But the great bulk of this, being without definite purpose, would be better named "ruminating". If, however, you desire to be a human being whose opinions and views are of any positive value it is imperative that you should learn, not merely to ruminate, but to "think out". If you try to remember what you had for breakfast you are certainly thinking, and it would be an entirely harmless occupation; but if you are a housekeeper, and in these difficult days had to solve the problem of to-morrow's breakfast, then you would be "thinking out". It is in this latter sense that the word is to be used in this talk, since it is in that sense we use the word when we call a man a "thinker", postulating that he uses his intellect to attack problems.

One of the main purposes of Education is to ensure that as large a number of people as is possible shall grow up "thinkers out" and not mere "ruminators". It would be difficult to believe that the Goddess of Learning is gratified with her success in this respect, although in the case of each individual so many years are devoted to the effort. If those years have, in the case of any one of you, failed to make you thinkers it would be ridiculous to suppose that, in one more hour, the want of success is likely to be retrieved. But your education does not end when you leave school—it would be truer to say that it begins then—and you will be educating yourselves, willy-nilly, all your lives; and it is possible, even in one hour, to tell you of a few elementary misconceptions about thinking which may hitherto have been obstacles in the path of your progress.

(1) True thinking is arguing with yourself. Your object, if you are as honest as you would claim to be, is one simple thing: to arrive at the truth, or at a working-hypothesis as near to the truth as, for the time being, you can penetrate. Try to blot out from your memory all those so-called arguments you must have heard in which two cocksure partisans have simply insisted impatiently each on his own point of view; such bickerings are wrangles, not arguments. When you yourself are confronted by a problem imagine that two counsel, for the prose-

cution and defence, are impartially presenting their case before you, and pointing out the holes in that of their opponent; with your own judgment as the tribunal, vowed to pronounced a verdict in accordance with the evidence.

In talking to you about Apperception I tried to impress on you the duty of keeping your apperception-masses fluid and receptive throughout your lives. The moment you cease doing so, stagnation sets in, and stagnation is intellectual death. One of your apperception-masses is your Conscience, another is your "artistic Conscience"; and what a great thinker (W. K. Clifford) said about the former, you can apply to the latter:

"I cannot believe that any falsehood whatever is necessary to morality. It cannot be true of my race and yours that to keep ourselves from becoming scoundrels we must needs believe a lie. The sense of right grew up among healthy men, and was fixed by the practice of comradeship. It has never had help from phantoms and falsehoods, and it never can want any. By faith in man and piety towards men we have taught each other the right hitherto; with faith in man and piety towards men, we shall nevermore depart from it. . . . It is wrong, always, everywhere, and for any one, to believe anything upon insufficient evidence. If a man, holding a belief which he was taught in childhood or persuaded of afterwards, keeps down and pushes away any doubts which arise about it in his mind, purposely avoids the reading of books and the company of men that call in question or discuss it, and regards as impious those questions which cannot easily be asked without disturbing it—the life of that man is one long sin against mankind."

(2) When you have reached a verdict on any question you must accept it unswervingly, and act upon it until such time as new evidence compels you to reopen the matter and stage a new trial. Do not fail, however, to consider searchingly the implications of your verdict; for it is in this opening of new avenues of thought that all the virtue of any knowledge consists. You will see the bearing of this from an instance. In a class on Acoustics we were recently dealing with the Velocity of Sound. The students were told that it was roughly 1,100 feet per second; and as a contrast they were told that light travelled at the colossal speed of 186,000 miles per second, and the even more astonishing fact that some stars are so far away that their light takes 2,000 years to reach us; which means that if the star suddenly exploded and ceased to exist at this moment, our astronomers would still be able to see it for the next 2,000 years. Many of the class were interested, wrote the facts down carefully, and asked me to repeat the figures for check-

ing; and they were possibly pleased to feel that they had a little more information to-day than yesterday. But few of them can have seen the implications, for they were clearly incredulous when I pointed out that, if an astronomer on that star had a telescope powerful enough to enable him to see what was happening on this earth, and was actually at that moment looking at us, he would behold the events which occurred here 2,000 years ago; which means that, a year or so from now, he would see Julius Cæsar landing in Britain. To realize this is to get an inkling of the importance of the observer without which one cannot even begin to understand the basis of the Theory of Relativity; for what would be the use of telling that astronomer that the event he was witnessing with his own eyes—not a copy, or a photograph, or any kind of reproduction, but the genuine first-time actuality—happened 2,000 years ago?

(3) Do not grudge time given to thinking out things, as if it was the same thing as day-dreaming. There are Eastern Races with whom a daily seclusion for meditation is a traditional habit; and though you may think that a counsel of perfection, there are nevertheless innumerable periods of the day when most of us do little but ruminate. If it took you an hour this morning to come here from your home, how was your mind occupied? "You have a long way to walk back", said a friend to a philosopher. "No", was the reply, "I just start thinking about something, and find myself at my front door." The Old Testament prophet tells us that the wisdom of a learned man cometh by opportunity of leisure; but the aphorism is not altogether true. To acquire his learning he must have set apart much time, but even a crowded day will provide a wise man with many opportunities for reflection. "Why are you idling?" said Emerson's mother to her son. "I am not idling, I am storing energy."

(4) In talking about Explanation you may remember my telling you that all teaching necessarily begins with definition. You must know what a word means, and how a thing is named, before you search for further knowledge. So begin your serious thinking with over-hauling words in common use, and see whether your apprehension of them is genuine or shallow. I have, for example, already pointed out to you that the answer to the question "Is England musical?"—often debated with some heat—depends solely on the meaning you give to the word musical. The shallow meaning is "fond of music", and the answer would be yes; the true meaning is "fond of good music", which immediately puts a question-mark to your answer. Make a list of

words which you use over and over again, and the next time you spend
ten minutes in an omnibus try to think out one of them. Here are some
ideas to start with:

(a) What is the real difference between a professional and an
amateur? Does not your mind immediately turn to the shallow explanation of money-payments? Two definitions have been made which
may help you to think deeper than that:

"An amateur can be satisfied with knowing a fact; a professional
must know the reason why."

"An amateur practises until he can do a thing right, a professional
until he can't do it wrong."

(b) What is Criticism?

"A man is a better critic of a thing than you are, if he can point out
to you some beauty in it which you had missed."

"If you say you like or dislike a thing you are not criticizing. Criticism begins with the word Because."

(c) What do you mean by Success?

"Success is the ratio between what you are and what you might
have been."

"Success is not beating other people; it is beating yourself."

(5) There are two methods of thinking, and you should always be
aware which you are using. The first, which logicians call Deduction,
starts with a law or conviction, and in the light of that judges a given
instance. "I'm a modernist, so I maintain that if it's by Scriabin it
must be first rate." Deduction may have its uses, but it has been for all
time one of the heavier curses laid on mankind, for by its opening statement it avows that the Court is prejudiced. Every progressive step in
the world's history, in every branch of human activity, has been met
point-blank by a major premiss which outlawed it. It is the only method
ever used by people who are too lazy to think. The second method,
called Induction, is that of Science: the collection of instances until
there emerges from them something near enough to a general law to be
available as a working-hypothesis. Use Deduction by all means—one
has to—for the smaller things in daily life, with the proviso that your
opening statement is your opinion and has not the authority of the
tablets of Sinai. But let all your real thinking be an effort to reach Truth,
not to proclaim that you have found it.

(6) We all could enumerate a number of qualities which we admire;

qualities which, if we could be born again, we would wish the fairy-godmother to insert in our make-up. Even if you keep this list a secret in your heart, you should nevertheless overhaul it periodically, and see if growing wisdom suggests amendment. I expect most of you would, for example, like to be quick, and you may be surprised to be told that in doing so you are unwise. The whole world, you will tell me, looks down with a touch of pity on the slowcoach. But hear what that great writer and thinker, Walter Savage Landor, has to say about it:

"Quickness is amongst the least of the mind's properties, and belongs to her in almost her lowest state; nay, it doth not abandon her when she is driven from her home, when she is wandering and insane. The mad often retain it; the liar has it; the cheat has it; we find it on the racecourse and at the card table; education does not give it, and reflection takes away from it."

I have known a good number of men with first-class minds; but though many of them, perhaps most, could be reasonably quick under pressure, I have never known one who resorted to speed when there was a possibility of reflection. This was one characteristic that made them first class. Do not be unreasonably hesitating or slow, or you will be bound to "miss the bus"; but no one ever caught an intellectual or artistic bus by galloping after it.

(7) A phrase has become current in recent years that has always filled me with some alarm: "the will to believe." It may, of course, carry a meaning that is not on the surface. For if one sees a thing is true, one will straightway believe it. If one does not see it is true, but would like to believe it—and such a case is easy to imagine—then to bring the Will into action seems to be merely tampering with the judge after the manner of Hitler in Belgium. I can understand any of you earnestly desiring to love your Bach, if you have not yet honestly reached that stage; and it is understandable if you feel it a stage you "ought" to and must reach, though I should much rather you said "hope" than "ought". The danger is that the sense of duty anticipates the flash of intuition. When anyone says "I simply adore the forty-eight" do you not suspect that they are boasting of having reached a goal that they have never set eyes on? If you have any artistic conscience, never pretend. Will to make the effort to appreciate all that is good and great, by means of the discrimination which you gain by thought and understanding. But do not let a sense of duty make you adopt the opinions of others, for that is pure stealing, and a sin against

H

your own mental and artistic growth. Do not aim at reaping your ideas from the golden harvest of another man's brain, but set to work rooting out the weeds and tares from your own.

(8) Lastly, there is an error in thinking, to which we are all liable, which has stunted the mental and artistic development of too many by leading them into a blind alley. It lies in mistaking the Means for the End. Have you never met the pundit who seems to know all the op. numbers in Classical Music? It is useful to know whereabouts in a list of, say, Beethoven's Sonatas a particular work may come; for one thing the knowledge will, or should, tell you to which "period" it belongs, for another you will be saved trouble in ordering a copy from a shop. But there are people who, as soon as you mention a work, fire off at you "Op. 127" as if it were proof positive of their own musical value—which, truth to tell, in such cases I have often found to be an imaginary quantity. Again, your work in Harmony and Counterpoint is inflicted on you in the hope that it will ultimately increase your musicianship; but in my young days the man who, often by very hard work, had mastered the intricacies of eight-part counterpoint, became a Mus.Doc., taught his pupils the tricks of the trade, and too frequently had no further traffic with the Art of Music.

The danger for performers lies in the parade of technique. In Chapter Four enough was said about the why and wherefore of technical skill, and I need only repeat that it is a means and not an end. If you are an artist you will know, in your heart, that when your listeners say how beautiful the music was, you have succeeded; when they only comment on how well you played or sang, you have failed. Do not the playing of fireworks, the insertion of the high note at the end of the song, and all such falls from grace, merely prove that the performer has not thought out the problem of the duty of an Artist to his Art?

CHAPTER FIFTEEN

THE MAP OF PSYCHOLOGY[1]

YOU must often have been told, in your school-days, that the whole is greater than its parts; though I doubt if the full implications of that statement occurred to you. An ocean is composed of drops of water; but a man might spend his life studying drops of water and yet die in ignorance of all that the word ocean means. Every component part of a building might be spread out before you in a builder's yard, but you cannot see the building, for it is something more than the sum of its parts.

The talks to which you have listened have put before you many apparently isolated facts and principles, and they must often have been already familiar to you, and may sometimes have seemed rambling and discursive. In this final lecture we have to see if they can be fused and welded together into a coherent plan, if we can make an ocean or an edifice out of our fragments. If in the end you see that the facts and principles do come together and form a whole, that properly strung the isolated beads will make a necklace, then you will have grasped—or apperceived—the meaning of the word Psychology.

When speaking to you about Education I told you of the Four Sides of Man; and now I want you to consider those sides again in relation to their fields of action, to the ends we strive to attain in each field, and to the methods which make it possible to reach those ends: that is to say the what, the why, and the how.

	Sides	Action	Aim	Means
A	Physical	The body	Reliability	Habit
B	Intellectual	Thinking	Wisdom	Understanding
C	Aesthetic	Feeling	Happiness	Control
D	Moral	Conscience	Character	Love of truth

[1] I cannot help feeling that psychologists in general will disapprove of this chapter, and even of its title. They are anxious nowadays to establish the fact that they deal with pure science, and will not willingly become ethical philosophers by considering aims and purposes. But I do not see, myself, how the application of psychology to educational purposes can be made unless we consider the aim of the teacher as well as the method he adopts.

A. The Physical Side.

In this category you can place everything that I have said to you about such things as Habit and Technique. To all of us here, as musicians, these two words, almost synonymous, are of superlative importance; and as this lecture is necessarily a summing-up, you must not resent a little recapitulation.

(1) Remember, then, above all things that your minds (and your pupils' minds) can only attend to one thing at a time. In performance, that one thing *must* be the musical interpretation, which must come straight from the heart, and must never be cut-and-dried. Consequently every movement of your arms, legs, fingers, and vocal cords must be automatic, to leave your mind free and unencumbered for the higher purpose. You may remember my calling your attention to one of the great mistakes we human beings continually make—the confusing of the end with the means. Wrestle out with yourselves what you honestly think to be the end of Technique. Is it not that the world may be able to see, when you no longer have to bother about accuracy, how interesting an interpreter you can be? Your first imperative obligation, as a performer, or conductor, or class-teacher, is to create a spell, and however gifted you may be all your nervous energy will be required for that. Once created, that electrical contact must be maintained at all costs, and you will inexorably find that the moment you switch your mind on to the "hard passage" the contact is broken; for the spell existed between your mind and theirs, and once broken, its recapture is next to impossible.

(2) Muscle-control is attained only by concentration of mind. It may need a thousand repetitions; but a million, without concentration, will not secure it. Girls have told me that, at school, they always practised their scales with a novel on the music-desk. I hope they derived some profit from the literature, for they could have gained little or none in any other way.

(3) Find out whether you—and each of your pupils—are of the kind to whom improvement comes gradually or in jumps. If you, or they, are in the latter class, cultivate faith by remembering that everything you can now do with ease and certainty was at one time a new and difficult problem. No technical difficulty I have ever been confronted with in music has filled me with such absolute despair as my first five minutes of learning to ride a bicycle.

(4) Do not let conscientiousness in your work drive you to ignore saturation point. The first sign of muscular fatigue is a hint to you that

the sponge is full; after that it is dangerous to risk strain, and foolish to waste time.

B. *The Intellectual Side.*

(1) Remember that improvement in one direction does not imply improvement in another. You may work at eight-part Counterpoint until it is child's play to you, or practise singing chromatic scales and shakes till the gallery marvels at your skill with open mouths: but you have only improved yourself in those particular lines. Your technique in two directions is greater than it was, but you are unwise to think you are therefore a better composer or a better Lieder singer: indeed, you will be a little lucky if you are not a worse. A fine mathematician is often a very indifferent bridge-player—even at adding up the score—and the best schoolboy chess-player I ever knew never succeeded in reaching the Upper School.

(2) Always search for a general rule, both in learning for yourself and in teaching others. If I were to ask you the sum of the first ten odd numbers, no doubt you could tell me in time, though some of you might want pencil and paper. Once you know the rule that the sum is always the square of the number you take—in this case it will be 100— you are applying a principle instead of juggling with a lot of facts. I wonder if you have ever thought out, for instance, why the seven sharps in a key-signature *had* to come in that order and no other; why the order of the seven flats *had* to be the exact reverse and could not have been otherwise; why you are asked, if your melody begins with an incomplete bar, to make your last bar correspondingly incomplete.

(3) Closely allied with the above, though it may sound more alarmingly philosophical, always try to get at the universal from the particular. That is one of the things which Algebra tries to do, as opposed to Arithmetic. The latter says that if apples are "two a penny", and you spend threepence, you will get six apples. Algebra, to get at a truth independent of two and three and six, says if apples are x a penny, and you spend y pence, you will get xy apples. If I asked you for an example of a major key-chord you might say C.-E.-G. or D.-F$\sharp$.-A., or any other—all particular cases., If you said "Tonic, mediant, dominant", you have expressed it "universally" because it is true whatever note the Tonic happens to be. Solfa-ists introduce children to a great musical truth, expressed in terms of the universal, by teaching them to sing Doh-mi-soh on any sound they may happen to hear, for they are teaching a universal idea instead of a particular application of it.

(4) That *Interest* and *Attention* are things of the mind is a fact you probably never doubted; and I am sure you will accept the psychologist's claim that unless you can evoke them your teaching will prove arid and worthless. You also knew, before listening to me, that a dull thing will become interesting if the right link can be found: how such an intrinsically dull thing as a postage-stamp can rivet the attention of a collector. But perhaps you did not realize that, even in the dullest incidentals of teaching, a link can and must be found; and that want of interest and attention in the pupils is, always and everywhere, to be attributed to the teacher.

In these two fields, the Physical and Mental, cleverness and quickness are due either to rapidity of sensation, as in reading, or of association, as in memorizing. But such cleverness, though it unfortunately often carries off the prizes, is not necessarily deep-seated. I remember once, when trying to solve a crossword puzzle, being beaten by a clue which I then read out, asking for help: "Give me a kiss and I can —— seven letters". In less than two seconds a quick-witted boy—otherwise rather unintelligent—gave the answer—Mexican. I confess that I felt anyone with such a quick working brain should have reached a higher intellectual status than this boy; then I remembered the quotation I have given you from Landor, and realized that to assume that Nature intended the boy to be a scholar was as rash as to assume that a child who happens to be endowed with "absolute pitch" should therefore devote its life to music.

C. The Aesthetic Side.

This, as I told you, is the realm of the Feelings and the Imagination; and the field includes all that will add to, or subtract from, the sum of human happiness.

(1) The intensity with which we feel, though it does vary from man to man, is not to be judged superficially. Some people's emotions respond to a hint: the very thought of misfortune makes them sad and sympathetic. Others have to be worked up, often with difficulty. But the time-factor is not the true test. "Depth of feeling" is not necessarily to be attributed to those whose eyes quickly fill with tears nor imperviousness to those who do not readily display emotion.

(2) Control of our feelings should be as fixed a goal as control of our muscles; and with honesty of purpose it is equally within our reach. Not, as a rule, in the case of congenital likes and dislikes, though even these have their variations from time to time, and sometimes prove

impermanent and modifiable. If you happen to dislike beer, as I do, it is improbable that any amount of determination will make you like it —even if you can think of any reason why you should embark on the effort. Yet when, during the 1914-18 war, I had a spell of work as an agricultural labourer, I discovered that, after a long session of digging, the one and only craving of my soul was for beer. Soon after peace the old dislike returned, and though I am sorry to have lost a capacity for enjoyment, I have acquired, I hope, a certain sympathy and under-standing.

Taste, in the sense of discrimination, has been defined as Thought guiding Feeling; and the definition is in itself an assertion of the possibility of control. An almost casual remark of Sir Walter Parratt influenced me, as a student, more than I can say. "Sometimes I find", he said, "that I dislike a passage in Brahms"; then he quickly added " But I always know it is my fault". If you steadily and fervently aim, on such occasions, at discovering why the composer put those notes on paper, you will generally end, with a little wholesome humiliation, by wondering at your own original lack of imagination.

(3) Remember, in this realm of the Feelings, that pleasure and happiness are not to be truly measured by quantity but by quality: not by amount, but by depth. If you are fond of cigarettes, and are a judge of them, would you rather have a single first-class one, or a dozen poor specimens? If you understand cricket, would you rather see Bradman bat for five minutes, or watch me do it for an hour? Happiness is a frame of mind, not a thing to which standards of measurement can be applied: pleasure is an incident, being your reaction to a stimulus. And I think all of us would rather be deeply touched for a moment, than made to purr for ten minutes.

To any artist the importance of the Imagination is self-evident and axiomatic, and I would like to give you two quotations from writers who were not themselves professional artists, which may help to strengthen your case when you speak with our enemies in the gate.

Einstein once said "Imagination is more important than know-ledge; for knowledge is limited, but Imagination encircles the world."

And another scientist said—

"Experience without Imagination is sterile. Imagination can make the prisoner in his cell dream dreams, and then, taking his pen, write the *Pilgrim's Progress*; it can make us poor human beings become only a little lower than the angels; it can stand at the bedside of the humblest drudge and say 'Get up, for to-day there are to be visions'."

D. The Field of Morals.

You will have seen, I am sure, that Psychology inevitably leads us to a point where we are face to face with Morality. That lies outside the range of anything about which I am supposed to talk to you. But taking the word in its broadest sense of "character" there are facets which the artist should recognize as affecting his work.

Your own personal morality—in the sense of character—depends solely on whether or no your Will obeys the dictates of your Conscience. But of all the millions who know this only individuals here and there seem to have perceived the inevitable corollary. Your conscience is a bundle of conclusions you have reached, drawn from experience, or instruction, or thought, as to right and wrong. So is the conscience of the first stranger you meet. But his bundle is entirely different from yours, and many things you may think perfectly right— say Sunday Tennis—he may think hopelessly wrong. That fact led the wise man to put my corollary into an aphorism: "Your first duty to your conscience is to educate it."

I would have refrained altogether from touching on Morality, even to this elementary extent, were it not that the "Artistic Conscience" is, in Music probably more than in other Arts, necessary to salvation. Of the outstanding importance of your character, I need only say that every time you go on a platform, every time you confront a class, your character will stand out in the limelight in everything you do or say. "It does not matter what you say to me", said Emerson; "What you *are* shouts so loud that I cannot hear your words." Another wise man said the same in other words: "The artist does not see things as they are, but as he is." I will not make a list of the many ignoble ways in which all performers are tempted to focus attention and applause on themselves. But I would like you, some day when you are in the mood for it, to ask yourselves one question, as an acid-test. If you had just finished your performance, and one of your listeners came up to speak to you, would you rather he said "How beautiful the music was", or "How well you did that". According to your answer you will know whether your artistic conscience is in need of further education.

The object of this talk has been, as you see, to try to knit together the strands of all the various things about which I have spoken to you, so that you might see that the isolated units can be brought together and fitted into a semblance of a mosaic of Psychology. I hope you have also noticed that, while trying to show you the applications of that Science to the Art of Music, I have also tried to establish the dignity of our Art, and its fitness for influencing the intellectual, the æsthetic, and even the moral side of man. It is for you to go out into the world with the resolve to maintain and further this dignity. To do so you must aim high: not for the sake of financial gain, nor for the gratification of the artistic temperament—a very different thing from the artistic conscience. You must do so because you realize, as a study of psychology compels you to realize, that Life is a bigger thing than any of its branches, including Music. So I will say farewell to you with a parable, leaving you to unravel its implications.

A great Cathedral was being built, and a visitor found himself in the yard where the masons carved their angels and gargoyles. Going up to a man he asked "What are you carving that for?" and the answer came "A pound a day". Going to a second mason he again asked why the man was carving his figure; and the answer came "Because I love carving". Of a third mason he asked the same question, and this time the answer was "Because I love Cathedrals".

Music will not make you rich, but it can make you happy; it will not save your soul, but it can make your soul worth saving. But the condition of both is that you should look on your careers not as pedlars having something to sell, but as idealists, trying to foster the world's imagination, and making the Art of Music subservient to the greater Art of Living.

WIDENER UNIVERSITY
WOLFGRAM
LIBRARY
CHESTER, PA

BIBLIOGRAPHY

For further reading the student will find any of the following works worthy of study:

T. P. Nunn: Education: its Data and first Principles.
P. Sandiford: Educational Psychology.
G. H. Thomson: Instinct, Intelligence and Character.
R. S. Woodworth: Psychology: a study of Mental Life.
Ll. Wynn Jones: Theory and Practice of Psychology.
R. M. Ogden: Hearing.
A. B. Wood: A Textbook of Sound.
J. H. Robinson: The Mind in the Making.
William James: Talks to Teachers on Psychology.
W. McDougall: Social Psychology.
D. C. Miller: A Science of Musical Sounds.
C. W. Valentine: The Psychology of Beauty (2nd Ed.).
M. Schoen: The Effects of Music.
C. E. Seashore: Psychology of Music.

INDEX

PRINTED IN
GREAT BRITAIN
AT THE
BOWERING PRESS
PLYMOUTH